NEW MEDIA

The Key Concepts

ISSN 1747-6550

The series aims to cover the core disciplines and the key cross-disciplinary ideas across the Humanities and Social Sciences. Each book isolates the key concepts to map out the theoretical terrain across a specific subject or idea. Designed specifically for student readers, each book in the series includes boxed case material, summary chapter bullet points, annotated guides to further reading and questions for essays and class discussion

NEW MEDIA

The Key Concepts

Nicholas Gane and David Beer

Oxford • New York

English edition
First published in 2008 by
Berg
Editorial offices:
First Floor, Angel Court, 81 St Clements Street, Oxford OX4 1AW, UK
175 Fifth Avenue, New York, NY 10010, USA

Berg is the imprint of Oxford International Publishers Ltd.

Library of Congress Cataloging-in-Publication Data

Gane, Nicholas, 1971-
    New media / Nicholas Gane and David Beer.—English ed.
        p. cm.—(The key concepts, 1747-6550)
    Includes bibliographical references and index.
    ISBN-13: 978-1-84520-132-6 (cloth)
    ISBN-10: 1-84520-132-9 (cloth)
    ISBN-13: 978-1-84520-133-3 (pbk.)
    ISBN-10: 1-84520-133-7 (pbk.)
    1. Mass media—Technological innovations. 2. Mass media—Social aspects.
I. Beer, David, 1977- II. Title.

P96.T42.G35 2008
302.23—dc22

                                                    2008025582

British Library Cataloguing-in-Publication Data

A catalogue record for this book is available from the British Library.

ISBN 978 1 84520 132 6 (Cloth)
        978 1 84520 133 3 (Paper)

Typeset by JS Typesetting Ltd, Porthcawl, Mid Glamorgan
Printed in the United Kingdom by Biddles Ltd, King's Lynn

www.bergpublishers.com

For Martha Beer, who was born during the writing of this book.

CONTENTS

ACKNOWLEDGEMENTS

We would like to thank Tristan Palmer, our editor at Berg, who had the initial idea for this project, and whose enthusiasm helped us (finally!) to produce this book. Roger Burrows offered valuable comments on a number of chapters of the manuscript, for which we are thankful. We would also like to thank Antonia Luther-Jones and Erika Deverall for their ongoing support.

Parts of Chapters 3 and 7 of this book have been reworked from the following publications:

Nicholas Gane, 'Speed-up or Slow Down?: Social Theory in the Information Age', *Information, Communication and Society*, 9(1) (2006): 20–38.
Nicholas Gane, 'Radical Posthumanism: Friedrich Kittler and the Primacy of Technology', *Theory, Culture and Society*, 22(3) (2005): 25–41.
Nicholas Gane, 'Simulation', *Theory, Culture and Society*, 23(2–3) (2006): 282–4.
Nicholas Gane, 'Posthuman', *Theory, Culture and Society*, 23(2–3) (2006): 431–4.

David Beer worked on the manuscript of this book while funded by the ESRC E-Society Programme.

1 INTRODUCTION: CONCEPTS AND MEDIA

Concepts are centres of vibrations, each in itself and every one in relation to all others.

Deleuze and Guattari (1994: 23)

The title of this book – *New Media: The Key Concepts* – appears self-explanatory. It suggests a book about the core concepts needed for the study of 'new' media technologies such as personal computers, MP3 players, mobile phones and other digital communications and storage devices. The quest for such concepts is indeed one aspect of the present work, but at the same time this book is no dictionary or encyclopaedia: it does not simply list concepts and definitions. Instead, it has a different purpose: to look, in particular, at six key concepts that facilitate theoretical and critical analysis of the new media age. The focus of this book is thus not simply the technical workings of new media technologies, although these will be touched upon in brief. Rather, the aim is to identify and define concepts for the analysis of emergent, highly technologized forms of social life and culture, and to look at how these concepts might be operationalized as *keys* for unlocking problems and barriers encountered in such research. The concepts to be studied here are: network, information, interface, archive, interactivity and simulation. It might be objected that by focusing in detail on only six concepts this book is a partial account, for many other concepts are needed for a comprehensive understanding of the new media age. This, of course, is true. But it is our belief that the six concepts chosen for study in this book are among the primary concepts required for this purpose. Together, when placed into contact with each other and also other concepts both old (such as power) and new (such as protocol or posthuman), they form a basic framework for analysis of contemporary society and culture; one which is intended to be open-ended and provisional, and which calls for further work by its very design.

Concepts, however, are difficult things to study. Like technologies they are not static entities, and because of this they are hard to pin down and analyse. One reason for this is that all concepts, including those addressed in this book, have complex histories and are sites of fierce contestation both across and within disciplinary boundaries. This book seeks to give a flavour of this complexity by exploring the migration of a number of concepts (particularly information, network and interface) from computer or information science into the social sciences and humanities. It also charts the key struggles over definition and appropriation of these concepts that have taken place as a consequence. Even this exercise is more difficult than it might at first seem, for the six concepts addressed in this book are a complex mix of material forms (for example, networks, interfaces, archives and possibly information) and processes (simulation or interactivity) that have taken on a particular conceptual or metaphorical significance in recent social and media theory. A key task, then, is to see how these metaphors are constructed from and shaped by the material forms or processes they seek to comprehend, and subsequently how they function as rhetorical devices within different approaches to the study of new media. For while a number of these concepts are not new as such (particularly network and information), they have taken on new lives in a range of quite disparate theoretical writings on the digital age. What becomes clear is that concepts are never set in stone but are rather mobile devices (see Deleuze and Guattari 1994: 143; Urry 2000) that are formulated and applied in response to the problems of the day. This means that for concepts to be useful, they must be fast-moving and flexible, especially if they are to enable us to keep pace with the vast array of technological transformations that are shaping social life and culture today.

WHY CONCEPTS?

But why write a book about concepts and new media in the first place? The simple answer is that concepts are the basic tools of thought that enable us to study digital technologies as media, alongside the complex social and cultural transformations they either drive, are tied to or result from, depending on your viewpoint. Traditionally, concepts have been seen as tools of thought that belong to the discipline of philosophy, in particular that branch of philosophy known as epistemology, which deals with the underlying foundations and structures of knowledge. This viewpoint is shared by thinkers as far removed as Isaiah Berlin, who designated the subject matter of philosophy to be those 'permanent or semi-permanent categories in terms of which experience is conceived and classified' (1980: 9), and Deleuze and Guattari, who declared philosophy to be the 'discipline that involves *creating* concepts' (Deleuze and Guattari 1994: 5). The present work might, on this basis, be considered to be a work of media philosophy, for it addresses the key concepts needed for the study of the digital age. But this is only partly true, for conceptual work is not confined strictly to philosophy and has taken place in a number of other disciplines, most notably sociology. From its outset sociology has been driven by disputes over 'key' concepts such as class, race, ethnicity, gender and age, not to mention 'the social' (see Gane 2004). Today, concepts remain at the very heart of sociological debate. Ulrich Beck (2000), for example, has declared contemporary sociology to be overburdened with 'zombie concepts': classical concepts that live on in name but which died years ago in terms of their analytic usefulness. In Beck's view, new concepts are needed, or perhaps old ones are to be reconfigured if sociology and related disciplines are to be more in tune with our times. Beck himself offers some such concepts, most notably 'risk', 'reflexive modernity' and the 'cosmopolitan'. But our view in this book is that there are other, arguably more powerful concepts that today are informing sociology and media/cultural studies – concepts which Beck neglects. These include network, information, interface, archive, interactivity and simulation. These concepts form the focal point of the present book, but we do not intend to consider them in the abstract. Rather, we seek to examine the origins and formation of these concepts and, perhaps more importantly, to look at how they might be *applied* or put to work in the analysis of social life and culture today. For this reason, this work might more accurately be called an exercise in *media sociology* rather than media philosophy.

This idea of putting concepts to work, however, is again more complex than it might first appear. For as Deleuze and Guattari (1994: 10–12) usefully observe, concepts may be produced for quite different reasons and applied in a variety of different ways. Deleuze and Guattari narrow these down to three main types of conceptual work. The first involves the manufacturing of what they call *universal* concepts. These are encyclopaedic definitions that seek to give concepts a fixed, universal meaning. While such definitions have their uses they are at the same time problematic, for concepts and their meanings are never completely stable. Concepts tend to mutate across time and between different cultural contexts, not least when they enter into mass circulation and take on meanings far removed from those originally intended. For this reason, just as Bruno Latour (2000) talks of 'recalcitrant objects' it might equally be possible to think of recalcitrant concepts: concepts that make thought possible but at the same time are hard to pin down and analyse. Concepts are sites of contestation, and because of this are likely to possess multiple meanings that cannot be reduced to a single straightforward definition. Deleuze and Guattari express this complexity in the following way: 'There are no simple concepts' for 'every concept is at least double or triple' (1994: 15). The concept of information used by a programmer facing an engineering problem, for example, is likely to be quite different to that advanced by a sociologist studying 'information society' (see **Chapter 3**). This, in turn, might appear to pose a problem for the present work, for the idea of 'key' concepts seems to imply the production of totalized concepts that are universal in application and singular in definition. This, however, is not the aim of this book, which seeks rather to work with concepts that are multifaceted and difficult by nature. The aim is not to simplify concepts by reducing them to a single meaning or form, but to work with their cross-disciplinary and historical complexities. The excitement of the present work is to see what happens when the double or perhaps triple meanings of concepts are forced to meet each other, not in an attempt to restore coherence to their multiple and fractured parts, but to see what creative possibilities might emerge precisely from such internal inconsistencies and frictions.

Second, concepts can be produced in service of the capitalist market. Deleuze and Guattari (1994: 11) talk, for example, of 'marketable' concepts: concepts geared to the production of ideas that are valued purely for their economic worth. An important extension of this process is the emergence of 'concept-driven' brands (see Klein 2000: 24), which draw their value less from the physical aspects of commodities than from the concepts that underpin and justify their design. Such concepts quite often have little to do with the materiality of their associated objects (for example, the concept of 'successful living' and the materiality of a pair of Diesel jeans), but work rather through the production of signs that are designed to sell an idea or lifestyle. This shift from the consumption of commodities valued because of their use-value or function to the production and consumption of signs, brands or ultimately *concepts* has been well documented by thinkers as far removed as Jean Baudrillard (1993a) and Naomi Klein (2000). But alongside this there is a further and perhaps more worrying aspect of this process: the penetration of creative thought more generally by the forces of advanced market capitalism. The commodification of knowledge has long been a target of critical philosophy – from Georg Lukàcs and the Frankfurt School through to 'postmodern' thinkers such as Jean-François Lyotard (see Gane 2003) – but today is intensified through the commodification of almost all scientific and artistic inventions. This process has been cemented in turn by the emergence of new forms of intellectual property (see Haraway 1997). Nigel Thrift also observes (2005: 4) that 'capitalist firms have taken on some of the language and practices' of social and cultural theory, and this has given rise in turn to new forms of 'knowing capitalism'. Deleuze and Guattari anticipated this situation, and respond to it with disdain: '[T]he more philosophy comes up against shameless and inane rivals and encounters them at its very core, the more it feels driven to fulfil the task of creating concepts that are aerolites rather than commercial products' (1994: 11). For them, the task of philosophy is to create concepts that are not tied to instrumental purposes or to economic value, and for this to happen a space for critical thought must be found outside of the logic and forces of capitalist culture.

This feeds into a third possible line of conceptual work that Deleuze and Guattari (1994: 12) themselves advocate, and which they term the '*pedagogy* of the concept'. This type of conceptual work is experimental in nature and uses concepts in a flexible, open-ended way to address research problems as and when they arise. Deleuze and Guattari declare that 'A concept requires not only a problem through which it recasts or replaces earlier concepts but a junction of problems where it combines with other coexisting concepts' (1994: 18). The 'junction of problems' that forms the focus of the present study is the analysis of the social and cultural dynamics of the new media age. As Deleuze and Guattari suggest, there is not a simple concept that will serve this purpose, but rather a network or plane of concepts that feed into and play off each other, in this case the concepts of network, information, interface, archive, interactivity and simulation. The idea is not to rank these concepts in terms of a hierarchy of usefulness but rather to use them as what Donna Haraway (2004: 335) calls 'thinking technologies' in order to describe and assess some of the key social and cultural transformations of our times.

One thing that soon becomes apparent is that many of the concepts addressed in this book are already powerful generators of ideas, particularly in the recent literature on *network* society (Castells 1996), the *information* age (Castells 1996, 1997, 2000a), *information* society (Webster 2002; Mattelart 2003), *interface* culture (Johnson 1997), and *archive* fever (Derrida 1996). In each of these cases, there is an intriguing feedback loop between concepts and the 'realities' they are attempting to comprehend. For if concepts are used to pose questions about the world around us, they have some kind of connection to this world even if they remain tools of thought. At the turn of the nineteenth century many neo-Kantian thinkers, including the sociologist Max Weber, addressed this question by arguing for a clear break between reality and concepts, but at the same time added that it is only through the use of concepts that we can hazard an understanding of reality, even if this is so complex it can never be known in any exhaustive sense (for an overview, see Burger 1976; Oakes 1988; Drysdale 1996). The logical outcome of this position is that the concepts that form the basis of analysis have to have some direct relation to the world of lived experience, and, more specifically, are to be chosen in the light of our individual research interests (what Weber called *Wertbeziehung* or value-relevance). Deleuze and Guattari say something similar: 'All concepts are connected to problems without which they would have no meaning ...' (1994: 16). For Deleuze and Guattari (1994: 20), concepts are those points around which the constituent components of thinking coincide, condense or accumulate. They consequently view them as 'anenergetic' forms: mechanisms or channels for releasing energy (very often libidinal) into intellectual and imaginative practice. In their reading, concepts have an incorporeal existence ('even though they may be incarnated or effectuated in bodies' (Deleuze and Guattari 1994: 21) and are neither essences nor things in themselves, but rather *intensities*. What unites neo-Kantianism with the wilder and more experimental philosophy of Deleuze and Guattari is that these intensities condense around *problems*. Problems prompt and stimulate conceptual work, and with this give it its value and meaning. Problems also tend to call into question knowledge in ways that cannot easily be assimilated within the existing order of things, and for this reason demand new ways of thinking, as theorists as far flung as Kuhn (1996) and Lyotard (1984) have shown. It is in this way, for Deleuze and Guattari, that concepts can assume a pedagogical role.

WHAT ARE 'NEW' MEDIA?

This book, then, is about the key concepts needed for the study of new media, concepts that to some degree might be drawn from the very technologies that are being placed into question. But what exactly are new media? An initial distinction may be drawn between *digital* communications media and older *analogue* technologies. This distinction, however, has been the subject of fierce debate within the discipline of media studies, not least because the apparent 'newness' of computer-based technology has been disputed on the grounds that there are important points of continuity between analogue and digital media (see Bolter and Grusin 1999). A central figure here is Lev Manovich (2001), who has argued that the technologies of early cinema anticipated many of the traits that are supposedly unique to digital media (see **Chapter 6**). For example, he argues that it is wrong to see old media as processing *continuous* data (data not composed of indivisible units) and new media *discrete* data (data made up of distinct units, such as pixels or bytes) because cinema worked at its outset by simulating movement through the processing of thousands of discrete images. Manovich does concede, however, that there is one fundamental difference between new and old media forms: the former operate through processes of 'numerical representation' while the latter do not. What makes new media 'new', for him, is that they operate through the production and processing of numerical (predominantly binary) code. This might not seem much in itself, but the consequences of this development are far-reaching, not least because the representation of cultural forms (including art, music, text) in numerical codes enables them to be reproduced, manipulated and transmitted with unprecedented ease.

One peculiar aspect of Manovich's *Language of New Media* is that it says remarkably little about either the connectivity of new media or the striking differences (as well as continuities) between the worlds of analogue and digital media. For this, a basic text such as Tony Feldman's *Introduction to Digital Media* is useful. Feldman opens this work by outlining a number of key traits of digital media. In particular, he argues that such media make information increasingly manipulable, networkable, dense, compressible and impartial. These traits are worth considering through the use of some everyday examples. First, digital media make possible the manipulation of data to an unprecedented degree, for such media work through the representation of information in an underlying code that can, as long as it is not protected in some way, be easily altered. Think, for example, of the difference between a typewriter and a word-processor. A typewriter physically stamps words onto a page, and because of this it is difficult to change what has been inscribed. But with a word-processor, words that appear on the screen are never set in stone because they are representations of an underlying digital code that can be manipulated at the touch of a button. The same differences mark out film-based from digital cameras. The former capture discrete images onto a film that is then difficult to change. But with the digital camera, there is no film, just a string of 0s and 1s that make up a digital image. Such images can be changed at will by manipulating this underlying code, something that becomes possible through the use of software suites that enable one to zoom into sections of the image, add filters and even introduce lighting from different angles. This heightened manipulability of information or data has led many to argue that digital technologies are by nature *interactive* media (a concept that will be explored in **Chapter 6**). Feldman says something similar: 'The fact that media are manipulable at their point of their delivery means something quite extraordinary: users of the media can shape their own experience of it' (1997: 4).

The second main feature of digital media is that, assuming a suitable protocol can be established, they can be *interfaced* with one another, and be connected through *networks* that span vast geographical spaces with relative ease. This is something we might take for granted today, but nevertheless is a defining feature of 'new' media: that 'information in digital form can be shared and exchanged by large numbers of users simultaneously' (Feldman 1997: 6). This has far-reaching implications, not least for the workings of capitalist culture. This can be illustrated through the use of an everyday example. A paper copy (old media) of the present book is a slow technological form that is reproduced through the physical copying of the printed page, and then distributed through physical space to its reader. An electronic text, by contrast, is a fast technology that can be reproduced, exchanged and circulated almost instantly, and with comparatively little cost to the producer. Feldman summarizes this shift as follows: 'Simultaneous access to networked information means distributing the same underlying content product many times over without the difficulties and costs implied by shifting physical products through a supply chain. In other words, networks transform the economics of media distribution'

(Feldman 1997). This pattern of changing business networks has been drawn on by theorists such as Manuel Castells as a model for rethinking the basis of *social* networks (see **Chapter 2**). More specifically, Castells (2001) sees new media as a driving force for the emergence of contemporary social networks that are predominantly 'me-centred' rather than close-knit communal forms. But this is not a view that is shared by everyone, as others, including Rheingold (2000) and Wellman and Gulia (1999), have argued that the new media age is also characterized by the emergence of new, virtual forms of community. This is something we explore in more detail in **Chapter 5**, but either way it is clear that there is something new about networkable media, along with the social forms of which they are both a driver and an outcome.

The remaining features of digital media are more technical in basis, including the third trait, which is that the data which new media process are increasingly *dense*. Feldman explains: 'We can squeeze a lot of information in digital form into a small physical space. Much depends, of course, on the particular storage technology used … If we use a print-on-paper analogy, we can encode the contents of a small library on a compact disc and mail it around the world for the cost of a postage stamp' (1997: 6). This logic of miniaturization is possible because, fourthly, digital media work through processes of *compression*, which enable huge digital files to move through networks and be stored with ease. Today, following the emergence of Web 2.0 applications such as the online encyclopaedia Wikipedia, even the compact disc is becoming redundant as files are increasingly stored in remote locations and accessed only when necessary. Such developments are part of wider processes of miniaturization, including those predicted by Marshall McLuhan (1964), who foresaw the transformation of previous media forms into the content of so-called 'new' media. An example is the emergence of video in the late 1970s. Initially, video was a 'new' media form as it transformed both television and cinema into content. Digital technologies today take this process to an extreme and perhaps even to its endpoint, for computers now have the capacity to render *all* previous media forms as content, including the typewriter, fax, record player, radio, camera, television and video. The boundaries between these previously separable forms become increasingly blurred as these technologies can be contained within a single medium, and in some cases within a single computer-based application. A device such as RealPlayer, for example, is a radio, television, video and music player in one. What makes this possible is again the representation of media content in the form of binary code. Once coded, there is no essential difference between music, text, images or even speech, and for this reason Feldman, finally, terms digital media *impartial*. For there is now no need for a range of different technologies for the processing of different types of data. Rather, all that is required is a single, overarching meta-medium: the computer. And here a further, material process of miniaturization is taking place, for computational machines are decreasing in physical size while at the same time becoming more powerful and perhaps even intelligent in terms of their ability to process information (see **Chapter 4**).

THE CONCEPTS

It is the task of the present book to forge a set of concepts that enable analysis of the above features of new media through consideration of the social and cultural conditions of which they are a part and to which they give rise. The majority of the concepts discussed in this book – network, information, archive, interactivity and simulation – are well known in sociology and cultural studies, and are on the verge of becoming key concepts in these disciplines. The remaining one – interface – has, by contrast, made less of an impact to date, although it is currently arousing attention in the discipline of media studies. While there is no hierarchy to the concepts analysed in this book and certainly no meta-concept that synthesizes all others, a start needs to be made somewhere and this will be with the concept of network in **Chapter 2**. While there is a quite long history of thinking about social networks (see, for example, Bott 1957), our interest is primarily in the migration of a technical version of this concept from computer and information science into the social sciences and humanities from the mid-1990s onward. What is interesting is that in the process of this migration the concept of 'network' changed in its meaning, leading some (van Loon 2006) to label it a trope. This chapter, by way of response, will begin by looking at recent technical definitions of networks from within the discipline of computer science. In this discipline, a network, in its most basic form, is an infrastructure that connects computers and external devices together, and which, as a result, enables communication of, and access to, data. Such networks may be local, global, open or closed and may assume a range of different forms or *topologies*, including star, ring or fully-connected. One thing that is striking is that with its passage into the social sciences and humanities, this concern for topology, along with the structure, rules and compatibility of network design, has been largely displaced in favour of a (Deleuzian) view of networks as chaotic, decentred and rhizomic. The concept of 'network' has also been used to describe a new societal arrangement that is characterized by heightened individualism, the emergence of new forms of connectivity between people, media and objects across physical spaces, and the accelerated movements of a range of different entities across the globe. Against this backdrop, three key sociological approaches to networks will be considered in this chapter: first, the ideas of 'network society' and 'networked capitalism' forwarded by Manuel Castells; second, the social networking approaches of thinkers such as Barry Wellman and finally, the actor network theory of Bruno Latour and John Law.

Chapter 3 turns to the concept of information, which again is more complex than it might at first appear. This concept, in spite of being part of everyday language, is remarkably difficult to define, and even theorists of the so-called information age or information society (such as Manuel Castells) say little about what it actually means. By way of response, this chapter traces the concept of information back to the writings of Claude Shannon and Warren Weaver, who define information as a statistical measure rather than a material property. This approach has influenced media theorists as far removed as Marshall McLuhan and Friedrich Kittler, but has also been subjected to criticism by feminist writers, most notably Donna Haraway and Katherine N. Hayles, who see it as a mistake to separate out information from the medium or physical body in which it is instantiated. This criticism, which reasserts a materialist theory of information, is examined by thinking of information as a part of a wider, structural web of *informatics*. It will be argued, however, that a key weakness of recent materialist theories of information advanced by thinkers such as Hayles and Kittler is that they are formulated in abstraction from the underlying dynamics of capitalist culture and society. For this reason, ideas of information society (Manuel Castells), information commodification (Jean-François Lyotard), and information critique (Scott Lash) will be considered at length.

Chapter 4 addresses the concept of interface. In recent years this concept has taken on an increased analytic significance as sociologists and media theorists have sought to understand the complex and fast-changing relations between humans and machines, hardware (including bodies) and software, and material and virtual worlds. It will be argued in this chapter that the interface is a concept that works between and across these apparent dualisms by opening up a common point of access between what quite often appear to be incompatible systems. An interface can work at the level of thought (indeed the concepts of the present book are perhaps interfaces that bring together ideas from different disciplinary or discursive systems), but they also have important physical realizations. This chapter will look at how such realizations – including handheld devices (such as MP3 players and mobile phones) that operate through graphical user interfaces – are becoming increasingly ubiquitous in everyday life, while at the same time becoming ever more powerful devices for the processing, storage and communication of information. The work of thinkers such as Lev Manovich, Donna Haraway and William Mitchell will here be used to think of the interface as something more than simply a technical form. It will be argued that the interface, as a concept, can be used as a critical tool for thinking creatively about the space of possibilities that might result from the opening of seemingly closed systems onto each other while, as a material form, being able to tell us something about the changing connections between the borders and boundaries between humans and machines.

The archive is the subject matter of **Chapter 5**. Archives are storage media that record and reproduce forms of collective memory, and thus tell us something about the changing basis of contemporary social and cultural life. The key figures for thinking about archives to date have been the French philosophers Michel Foucault and Jacques Derrida. This chapter will argue that the work of these two thinkers is now outdated. Foucault sees archives as technologies that enable the storage and governance of written documents. This view of the archive is now far too narrow as it says little about the range of media that can be used to archive data, along with the different types of data that might be archived, including images (still and moving), sounds, numbers and text (see Kittler 1990). Derrida in one sense goes beyond Foucault by attempting to think about archives in the digital age, but like Foucault he restricts his analysis to e-mail – again a textual form. Of interest, however, is his attempt to trace the concept of the archive back to the Greek *arkhē*, which means both commencement (to make a beginning through an act of recording) and commandment (the government of this process). He also talks of the *arkheion*: the private and legally protected space in which public documents were originally housed. Against this turn back to Greek antiquity, we will argue that a more contemporary reading of archival technologies is needed for at least two reasons. First, with the emergence of new media archives that are accessible to the masses it is no longer the case that the archive simply contains public documents that are stored in private spaces. Increasingly, the reverse is true: private or personal documents, images and music files today saturate the public spaces of the Internet, particularly following the emergence of the user-generated world of 'Web 2.0'. This signals a basic shift in the underlying form of the archive as it has become increasingly *individualized*. Second, this situation has been accompanied by a change in the governance of archives and the data they store and transmit. For now, there is less of a 'gatekeeper' approach to public archives as these are often assembled through the collective work of individuals (for example, as wikis), and tend to be policed through the local and decentralized actions of their users (although this may well be starting to change).

Chapter 6 places the concept of interactivity into question. As stated above, it is commonly assumed that digital media are by their very nature interactive media, for they are seen to enable the unprecedented manipulation of data by lay users. However, the concept and reality of 'interactivity' have been hotly contested. One difficulty is that the concept of interactivity can be applied to the analysis of interaction not only between humans and machines but also between machines and machines and between humans and humans. This chapter will focus on human-computer interactivity as these other forms have dealt with in detail by, respectively, computer scientists and micro-sociologists. A key point of interest is just how interactive 'new' media are in comparison with their older, analogue counterparts. This question will be explored by constructing a dialogue between on one hand Lev Manovich who, as noted above, sees new media to be in some ways less interactive than traditional media forms such as books and paintings, and on the other Marshall McLuhan (1964), who sees new electric forms of media as requiring more 'filling in' and therefore as requiring a higher degree of interaction with their users. Analysis of these positions will in turn feed into a consideration of contemporary social theories of media interactivity, including those that have attempted to revitalize this concept by applying it to the study of communication, memory and recent notions of active citizenship. In the final section of this chapter, we also consider the interactivity of Web 2.0 applications that promote the mass production and consumption of user-generated content (something we also consider in **Chapter 5**), and which are tied to or perhaps give rise to new forms of intelligent or 'knowing' capitalism (Thrift 2005).

Finally, **Chapter 7** looks at the concept of simulation. This concept is most closely associated with the work of Jean Baudrillard, who analyses contemporary capitalism in terms of a culture of simulation that blurs the boundaries between what is 'real' and what is virtual or 'hyperreal'. This chapter will outline the basic features of Baudrillard's theory of simulation before looking in detail at more recent work by Friedrich Kittler and Katherine Hayles, both of whom emphasize the underlying materialities of the digital age. Kittler's main contribution is to draw into question the connection between software and the underlying hardware of media machines. His position is that today software increasingly operates according to predefined rules that are burnt into the chipsets of computational technologies. By implication this means that if we wish to understand the workings of simulated environments we must examine closely the machines that produce them. This, in turn, extends our previous consideration of the concept of interactivity, for Kittler argues that there is in fact little interactivity in mainstream digital media, as for the most part these run through graphical user interfaces that allow little manipulation of the structure of their underlying systems. Hayles also attacks Baudrillard for downplaying the material foundations of simulation technologies. Contrary to Baudrillard, she argues that 'computational engines and artificial intelligences' can never be treated simply as virtual or simulated forms for they cannot work without 'sophisticated bases in the real world' (Hayles 2002: 6). In line with this statement (and her theory of information, see above), Hayles talks not of computer simulation or hyperreality or of the possibility of downloading mind or consciousness into a machine (see, for example, Moravec 1999), but rather of *embodied virtuality* (which distances her from Kittler), and of new forms of subjectivity that might be born out of the interface between human bodies and computer-based technologies. We will address this connection between (bodily) matter and the virtual in further detail through consideration of recent ideas of the 'posthuman'. This, in turn, is a fitting place to conclude this book, as the posthuman is currently a focal point for new and exciting debates over virtuality, embodiment, agency and information, and as such is becoming central to the concerns of new media studies.

Chapter Summary

- Concepts are basic tools of thought that enable us to address the underlying dynamics of the new media age.
- Concepts have complex and contested histories and because of this often have more than one meaning.
- Conceptual work may take different forms: encyclopaedic, market-driven and *pedagogical* (Deleuze and Guattari).
- There are important historical and technical connections between 'old' (analogue) and 'new' (digital) media technologies, and because of this the idea of 'new' media is contested.

2 NETWORK

> The network is the message.
>
> Castells (2001: 1)

'Network' is the first of the six concepts we analyse in this book. We have chosen to open with this concept with the aim of forging a basic infrastructure of ideas that will help underpin analysis of the five other concepts considered in this book. But this is by no means an easy place to start, for the concept 'network' has a long and complex history that may be traced back through a number of different academic disciplines, including anthropology, economics and sociology. (For a comprehensive overview, see Knox et al. (2006) and Scott (2000: 7–37).) What interests us in this chapter, however, is the migration of concepts or metaphors of networks that, from the mid-1990s onward, passed from computer engineering into the social and cultural sciences and beyond into popular usage. But even with this restricted focus on network as a tool for analysing new media culture and society, the multiple meanings attached to this concept make it notoriously difficult to define and use. Network is not a concept that unites a shared vision of topology or connectivity across or even within disciplines. Rather it is a contested and 'uncanny' concept (Lovink 2002).

Joost van Loon reflects that as

> a term that has become an established element in the vocabulary of knowledge both inside and outside the academy, 'network' has a complex and inherently unmappable genealogy. This is because it is not simply a theoretical concept, whose origins can somehow be traced back to a particular original thinker. Instead, the usage of the concept of network is in the first instance metaphorical. It is a trope. (2006: 307)

A trope is a rhetorical device that shifts the use of a word away from its literal or original form. Network, at least in its contemporary usage, is a trope insofar as its meaning has shifted as it has passed from computer science (concerned with the engineering and analysis of connections between computers and various auxiliary devices) into the social sciences, where it has come to signify a new societal arrangement characterized by a culture of individualism and the accelerated mobilities of people, commodities, capital, signs and information across the globe. This chapter will attempt to explore this process of disciplinary migration by looking initially at the physical design of new media networks. This will give us a basic technical outline of what such networks are and of the different physical forms or topologies they may take. Three key sociological and philosophical approaches that have utilized the concept of 'network' will then be considered: first, the idea of 'network society' or 'networked capitalism' that is most prominent in the writings of Manuel Castells; second, theories of 'social networking' that have re-emerged in recent studies of the uses of information communication technologies, most notably in the work of Barry Wellman and John Scott; and finally, the actor-network theory of Bruno Latour and John Law (which has been inspired in part by the writing of Gilles Deleuze and Félix Guattari). What is interesting about these bodies of work is that although they were produced at roughly the same time – from the mid-1990s onward – there is little dialogue between them, and each occupies a different space within the discipline of sociology. The challenge this presents is to work across and between these thinkers in order to produce an open concept of network that might, in turn, be used to explore the underlying social and cultural dynamics of the new media age.

WHAT IS A NETWORK?

As stated in the introduction to this book, a defining feature of new media technologies is that they can be interfaced with one another and, because of this, operate within networks. William Mitchell, in his book *Placing Words*, observes that 'digital devices rarely operate in isolation, but are linked to one another by communication channels' (Mitchell 2005: 16), and together form digital networks that today are woven into the fabric of everyday life. If we are to address this situation we must first ask a basic question: what exactly is a new media network? A simple answer is that it is an infrastructure that connects computers to each other and to a range of external devices, and thereby enables users to communicate and exchange information. Networks, however, come in many shapes and forms. A computer network may be either localized (a local area network (LAN) or Ethernet), meaning that it 'covers a small geographic area and connects devices in a single building or group of buildings', or it can cover a 'larger area such as a municipality, state, country, or the world' (a wide area network or WAN) (Shay 1999: 8). Whether wide or local, a network is distinguished by an underlying architecture or *topology*. This can vary from very simple to very complex depending on the number of computers and devices that are connected, and, perhaps more importantly, on the way in which these connections are configured, arranged or 'assembled' (Latour 2005; DeLanda 2006).

In short, networks can be 'classified into broad categories according to their general shape' (Comer 2004: 107). The simplest arrangement is a star topology in which a single computer lies at the centre of a network, over which it subsequently establishes a high degree of control, for 'data transfers between terminals or between terminals and storage devices occur only through the main computer' (Shay 1999: 10). A ring topology, by contrast, connects computers and devices circularly so that a machine can only communicate through devices that are its immediate neighbours. This type of setup is common in the world of digital music, where instruments are placed into networks through a Musical Instrument Digital Interface (MIDI), which enables a master device to communicate information to attached slave units. Shay gives a further example: 'Ring topologies such as IBM's token ring network often connect PCs in a single office or department. Applications from one PC can thus access data stored on others without requiring a mainframe to coordinate communications' (Shay 1999: 12). There are also more complex network designs. For example, there is the possibility of a fully connected topology in which there is direct connection and communication between all devices in the network. Shay calls this an 'extreme' and costly system design because of the many connections that are required in such a system, many of which may well lie dormant in day-to-day use. For this reason, this network design is rarely operationalized. Finally, there are combined topologies – common to most Internet users today – that combine a number of these arrangements in complex systems architectures. This topology might include, for example, connections to a mainframe for data storage, a local network for communication within a locally defined group, and a range of different servers for Internet use.

The key point to take from this is that a network is not a single structural form, for in practice networks may have quite different architectures or topologies. Moreover, for any network to operate smoothly a set of standards or *protocols* is needed to enable different machines and devices to communicate with each other. Protocols are necessary to ensure compatibility between different media, particularly where networked devices may be products of different manufacturers. The important thing to consider here is that while computers are often thought of, in principle, as being much the same, in practice they 'have different architectures, understand different languages, store data in different formats, and communicate at different rates' (Shay 1999: 14). This poses a problem for the design of meta-networks such as the Internet – 'a global network of networks' (Walrand 1998: 22; see also Mitchell 2003: 9–10) – that connect together millions of machines and devices, for such devices need to be able to communicate with one another. The answer lies in the formulation of a basic set of meta-rules or protocols that enable open communication between different systems. Any Internet user will immediately recognize these as a series of acronyms that end in the letter p: ftp, tcp, ip and http, to name but a few. (See Comer 2004: 637–81 for a definition of these and others.) The function of such protocols is to create a standard format that enables information to be exchanged between different parties and across different platforms. Comer explains that

> All parties involved in a communication must agree on a set of rules to be used when exchanging messages ... Diplomats call such an agreement a *protocol*. The term is applied to computer communication as well: a set of rules that specify the format of messages and the appropriate actions required for each message is known as a *network protocol* or a *computer communication protocol*. The software that implements such rules is called *protocol software*. (2004: 252)

There is no single protocol for the governance of a complex network; rather there are *suites* of protocols that manage different aspects of the communication process. These protocols work by breaking down communication networks into different layers. The most famous model for doing this is the 'open systems interconnection reference model' (or OSI model), which was formulated by the International Organization for Standardization (ISO) in an attempt to promote and enhance

Case Study: MIDI

Networks are governed by protocols that enable new media devices to connect to one another and to communicate effectively. The digital music synthesizer is one such networked technology. In the early 1980s, the number of digital music synthesizers produced by different manufacturers proliferated, and compatibility became an increasingly significant issue — particularly when musicians tried to assemble networks of devices that had different internal principles of design. The manufacturers of these technologies responded by collaborating on the development of a Musical Instrument Digital Interface or MIDI: a protocol designed to ensure that devices made by different manufacturers are compatible. The major digital instrument manufacturers agreed to move forward with MIDI in January 1982. The protocol was drafted by September 1982, and the resulting interface was embedded into instruments by the end of that year. MIDI subsequently became an essential protocol in enabling networked musical devices to talk to one another, and for this reason helped shape the popular music scene from the early 1980s onward. Interestingly, MIDI is a voluntary protocol that manufacturers chose to follow, and is one that is still widely used today.

The development of digital music production and the associated desire to network devices (including internetwork compatibility. This model, which was first formulated in the late 1970s and which still informs Internet design today, divides network systems into seven distinct but interrelated layers. Shay outlines the basic logic of this model: 'Each layer performs specific functions and communicates with the layers directly above and below it. Higher layers deal more with user services, applications, and activities, and the lower levels deal more with the actual transmission of information' (Shay 1999: 17). For the most part, users will only be aware of the application layer that sits at the top of this chain, for this enables day-to-day operations such as e-mail and file transfers between servers and machines. But beneath this there are six further layers – presentation, session, transport, network, data link and physical (see Shay 1999: 20–3 for a description of these) – that compress data downward so that they can be sent through the physical hardware of a network and be reassembled at the other end with as little noise or deformation as possible. (On the question of noise see the opening section of **Chapter 3**.) Residing within each level of this structure are protocols that allow these layers to communicate with each other and thereby enable the system to work as a whole. To summarize: networks tend to have clear internal structures, and are governed, for the most part, by universal standards or rules, without which communication between different platforms and systems would be nearly impossible.

---

personal computers to control sequencing) highlights the issue of compatibility and the need for standards or protocols to ensure the operation of networks of instruments. Analogue synthesizers, despite some problems of controllability, were usually capable of some level of interaction and compatibility, even if this tended to be unpredictable. Incompatible digital devices were simply unresponsive so could not be 'patched' together in the same way. The advent of MIDI, and the overcoming of some of the more fundamental problems of cross-platform communication, proved crucial in the development of digital synthesis technologies. This illustrates the importance of compatibility and protocols in enabling the connections that structure new media networks. Understanding networks might require some sense of the history of the resolution and non-resolution of the problems and glitches around connectivity. MIDI is an example of collaboration between manufacturers to achieve compatibility. Elsewhere, we might look to identify where non-compatibility is used to create material barriers between networks and to defend and protect market territories. One example of such a barrier is the hard-wiring of mobile phones so that they can only be used with the networks of particular network providers (such as the iPhone and AT&T or O2).

NETWORK SOCIETY

Many of these basic properties of computer networks have been developed into metaphors for thinking about the day-to-day operation and underlying basis of contemporary capitalist society. The key thinker here is Manuel Castells, author of *The Rise of the Network Society* (1996), which is the first volume of his huge trilogy *The Information Age* (Castells 1996, 1997, 2000a). In the concluding chapter of *The Rise of the Network Society* (Castells 1996) and in a paper entitled 'Materials For An Exploratory Theory of the Network Society' (2000b), Castells outlines in detail how the concept of network might be useful for the analysis of contemporary social and cultural change. Castells starts by defining networks as emergent structures made up of a number of interconnected nodes, the character or topology of which may be very different depending on the type of systems of which they are part (for example, a stock exchange market or the political networks of the European Union, see Castells 1996: 501). The important move, for Castells, is to consider networks as *social structures*. He declares that 'Networks are open structures, able to expand without limits, integrating new nodes as long as they are able to communicate within the network, namely as long as they share the communication codes. A network-based social structure is a highly dynamic, open system susceptible to innovating without threatening its balance' (Castells 1996: 501–2). A network, then, is a structural form, but one that is quite different to the types of social structures common to the industrial societies of the nineteenth and early twentieth centuries. For while networks in themselves are nothing essentially new, Castells observes that they have taken on a new vitality in the information age, especially where they are 'powered by new information technologies' (2000b: 15). These technologies transform networks by enabling 'an unprecedented combination of flexibility and task implementation, of co-ordinated decision making, and de-centralized execution, which provide a superior morphology for all human action' (Castells 2000b: 15). This is a key statement, for it shows that Castells is less concerned with the technical, internal workings of networks than with developing the idea of a network into a metaphor that captures the technologized and transient basis of contemporary social relations. One consequence of this is that while Castells hints that networks may assume multiple topologies, in practice he tends to use the concept of network to symbolize a society that is increasingly de-centred, flexible and individualized. This means, in turn, that the idea of networks operating through hierarchical processes of control, as described in the technical network literature, is for the most part dropped in favour of a concept of the network as an 'open' and 'dynamic' system. (We address this in further detail below.)

This move subsequently underpins Castells' idea of 'network society': a societal form that is characterized by a transformation of lived time and space, and by the emergence of new 'timeless time' and 'spaces of flows'. Timeless time is an accelerated time that is unique to the new media age. It is a computerized time created by machines that operate and communicate with each other at speeds far beyond the sensory perceptions of their users. In more general terms, timeless time refers to a regime of instant communication and information exchange in which there is little time for reflection and perhaps critique (as suggested by Scott Lash, see the final section of **Chapter 3**). McLuhan anticipated this situation in the mid-1960s, as he saw electric technologies introducing a culture of immediacy in which 'action and reaction occur almost at the same time' (1964: 4). Castells adds, however, that this world of timeless time is accompanied by the emergence of a space of flows in which 'localities become disembodied from their cultural, historical, geographical meaning, and reintegrated into functional networks, or into image collages' (1996: 406). This space of flows is made up of key nodes and hubs, each of which has a clearly defined functionality and is connected through complex sets of relations. Castells gives the following example: 'Some places are exchangers, communication hubs playing a role of coordination for the smooth interaction of all the elements in a network. Other places are the nodes in the network; that is, the location of strategically important functions that build a series of locality-based activities and organizations around a key function in a network' (1996: 443). At this point, a network, for Castells, is no longer simply a metaphor of a new social arrangement, but is instead a distinct spatial form that is defined by the connections it forges between different physical nodes or places. The technical idea of a network as system architecture, as outlined in the opening section of this chapter, is here shifted into a geographical concern for social space.

The difficulty this presents is whether network is, for Castells, a concept or a tool for analysis or whether it is in fact a description of new societal and cultural forms, or perhaps both. This complex relation between conceptual work and empirical description is something we will return to in the conclusion to this chapter, but for now it is worth noting that there is perhaps a slippage between Castells' ideal-typical vision of the network as an open, decentred form and how network society operates in reality. In some respects, Castells' emphasis on the physicality of networks is not far from the technical definitions of networks discussed at the outset of this chapter, not least because it gestures toward the importance of protocols for the smooth running or perhaps even the governance of networks. In the passage quoted at the outset of this section, Castells observes that networks are open systems just as long as they 'are able to communicate within the network, namely as long as they share the communication codes' (1996: 501–2). This is possible only if a common standard or protocol is agreed upon to enable such sharing. Interestingly, Castells suggests that such protocols, and the points of interface between different networks, are today key strategic sites of control and power. He declares that 'Switches connecting the networks … are the privileged instruments of power. Thus the switchers are the power-holders. Since networks are multiple, the inter-operating codes and switches between networks become the fundamental sources in shaping, guiding and misguiding societies (Castells 1996: 502). Moreover, within networks there are locations of privilege on one hand and of marginality on the other. For while Castells argues that networks have no centre as such, some nodes within a network are more important than others, depending on the functions they serve.

Castells declares, however, that this skewing of networks is itself dynamic: 'no nodal domination is systemic. Nodes increase their importance by absorbing more information and processing it more efficiently. If they decline in their performance, other nodes take over their tasks' (2000b: 15–16). This emphasis on the absence of systematic domination, underpinned by a vision of networks as internally comp-etitive structures by nature, is perhaps surprising. For in practice, some degree of systemic privileging is built into most networks, be this through the privileging of certain points of access in data or communications networks, or the result of hist-orical and political forces that lead certain cities to be more influential than others in global financial networks. (For a discussion of cities and globalization see the opening chapter of Savage et al. (2005).) Castells does not analyse such structural forces directly, but questions the connections between networks, political authority and human agency. He asks, for example, 'who programmes the network?' and 'who decides the rules that the automaton will follow?' (Castells 2000b: 16). His answer in the first instance is 'social actors'. But, in practice, things are more complex than this, for he adds that 'there is a social struggle to assign goals to the network. But once the network is programmed, it imposes its logic to all its members (actors). Actors will have to play their strategies within the rules of the network' (Castells 2000b: 16). In view of this, networks are perhaps not as open, flexible and dynamic as Castells initially suggests.

Castells applies this theory of networks, in turn, to a description and analysis of contemporary capitalism. His starting point is the idea that network society is fund-amentally capitalist society (see Castells 1996: 502). He observes: 'Business firms and, increasingly, organizations and institutions are organized in networks of vari-able geometry whose intertwining supersedes the traditional distinctions between corporations and small business, cutting across sectors, and spreading along different geographical clusters of economic units' (Castells 1996). Perhaps more importantly, markets are now networks that are designed to enable flows of capital, information, signs and commodities across the globe with the least possible friction. Castells thus theorizes capitalism not as a single structural form but as a complex and dynamic *network of networks* – what Arjun Appadurai (1996) has called a 'scape'. A key feature of this argument is that networks share the same logic of performativity as that which lies at the heart of the capitalist system. Networks are conduits for the flows and exchange of capital, and because of this are designed to maximize the efficiency and profitability of the system of which they are a part. Castells observes that 'Networks converge toward a meta-network of capital that integrate capitalist interests at the global level and across sectors and realms of activity: not without conflict, but under the same over-arching logic' (Castells 1996: 506). Networks, for Castells, are very much part and parcel of the basic infrastructure of contemporary capitalist society and culture. For while they make new forms of accelerated capitalism possible they are at the same time directed by the basic principles of economic exchange and accumulation upon which these forms are based.

Castells illustrates this argument by drawing attention to the individualization of social relationships within what he calls 'network society'. In *The Internet Galaxy* – the first chapter of which is entitled 'The Network is the Message' – he argues that network society is founded upon a shift from communities, or close-knit social structures based on shared values and genuine interest in others (a view that some might see as being a little too romantic – see Bauman 2001a), to 'me-centred' networks, which are individualized social forms in which people position themselves in order to maximize personal gain. Castells explains: 'Communities ... were based on the sharing of values and social organization. Networks are built by the choices and strategies of social actors, be it individuals, families, or social groups' (2001: 127). This suggests that it is the performance-driven logic common to both technical and business networks which now shapes the basic structure of everyday social relations between humans. For Castells, a key feature of this development is that individuals increasingly place others into their social networks for their potential use rather than because of their intrinsic worth. Castells calls this 'a new pattern of sociability based on individualism' (Castells 2001: 130), and argues that computerized communication networks played a key role in its emergence. He reflects: 'it is not the Internet that creates a pattern of networked individualism, but the development of the Internet provides an appropriate material support for the diffusion of networked individualism as the dominant form of sociability' (Castells 2001: 130–1). Castells' argument is that new media, while not causing the rise of networked individualism, has provided the technical infrastructure for it to develop, be sustained and perhaps even intensified over time.

SOCIAL NETWORK ANALYSIS

This idea of social networking and of 'networked individualism' has been developed by a number of other thinkers alongside Castells. In contrast to more abstract visions of the network society, social network analysis (or SNA) has tended to take a more empirical approach toward understanding the ways in which actors operate and connect within networks. As Knox et al. (2006) and Scott (2000) point out, social network analysis has a long and complex history that clearly predates the new media age (see for example Bott 1957). The reason it is of interest to us is that a number of thinkers, most notably Barry Wellman, have attempted to apply such analysis to the relations forged through the usage of new media technologies, in particular the Internet. In the introduction to their collection *Social Structures: A Network Approach*, Wellman and Berkowitz define 'network analysis' as 'neither a method nor a metaphor, but a fundamental intellectual tool for the study of social structures' (1988: 4). On the surface, this approach seems close to that found in Castells' theory of network society. But in practice it is quite different, for the basic idea of network analysis is not to look at a self-contained network society per se, but to 'view *relations* as the basic units of social structure' (Wellman and Berkowitz 1988: 15). This means that network analysis does not start with a theory of groups or society, but instead proceeds by looking at the density and texture of relations or connections between nodes, which might include 'individual people ... groups, corporations, households, nation-states, or other collectivities' (Wellman and Berkowitz 1988). These connections, in turn, can be measured, modelled and visualized (see Scott 2000: 5), with the consequence that this approach tends to be quite mathematical in orientation (see for example Harrison White's analysis of markets (1988: 226–60)). This emphasis on mathematics, however, does not mean that social network analysis is simply a quantitative research technique, for a key point of interest of such analysis is the *quality* of relations that exist between nodes. Scott explains: 'While it is, of course, possible to undertake quantitative and statistical counts of relations, network analysis consists of a body of qualitative measures of network structure' (2000: 3). This in turn is important, for it gives us a detailed sense of the *social topology* of network society – something that, by contrast, is largely missing from Castells' work.

This is just one among several reasons for the revival of social network analysis in the new media age. First, the 'growth of the Internet as a communication medium has increased the opportunities for data collection of social network data' (Neustadtl et al. 2002: 199). This is not restricted just to the medium of the Internet, for the unprecedented processing power of computers today gives new means for the collection and manipulation of different forms of attribute, relational and ideational data (Scott 2000: 2–3). Indeed, in an appendix to *Social Network Analysis: A Handbook*, Scott (2000: 175–80) reviews some of the software packages that have made advanced social network analysis possible. Second, and perhaps more interestingly, there has been renewed interest in the definition and measurement of network relations in the light of the mediation of social life by information communication technologies such as the Internet. A key text here is the edited collection by Barry Wellman and Caroline Haythornthwaite (2002) entitled *The Internet in Everyday Life*. This book draws together a range of studies that explore how Internet use fits into established everyday activities and practices, many of which are concerned with the social aspects of networks and networking. The collection describes a period in which the Internet became an everyday technology and took on an increasingly significant role in social relations of various types, including those between individuals and between individuals and organizations. This approach calls into question exactly how technologies such as the Internet become embedded into our social worlds, and looks at the complex networks of relations which emerge as a result. Wellman and Haythornthwaite's basic position is that we 'cannot understand the relations of two people – or a small group – online without considering the broader social networks in which they are connected, offline as well as online' (Wellman and Haythornthwaite 2002: 35). Online relations, then, are not disconnected from life in the so-called 'real world', but are rather to be understood as one part of a much wider set of socially networked relations in which individual users are located.

To put this simply, online networks are never divorced from the social networks that make up the mundane realities of everyday life. Wellman and Haythornthwaite offer the following reflection:

> The Internet has continued this turn towards living in networks, rather than in groups. In such networked societies, boundaries are more permeable, interactions are with diverse others, linkages switch between multiple networks and hierarchies are flatter ... Their work and community networks are diffuse and sparsely knit, with vague, overlapping, social and spatial boundaries. Their computer-mediated communication has become part of their everyday lives, rather than being a separate set of relationships. The security and social control of all-encompassing communities had given way to the opportunity and vulnerability of networked individualism. People now go through the day, week, and month in a variety of narrowly defined relationships with changing sets of network members. (Wellman and Haythornthwaite 2002: 33)

This, in turn, has implications for an understanding of what is meant by the idea of community. As stated above, Castells theorizes the emergence of network society in terms of the transition from communal forms of existence, in which individuals are tied to others through strong social bonds that are often forged through physical proximity, to new forms of me-centred networks in which individuals position themselves to maximize their personal gains from others. By contrast, in the work of Wellman and Berkowitz, community itself is read as a form of network. This is because, for them, what matters is the quality and density of relations along with the connection and positioning of such relations within broader social networks. They state that

> Recent work on communities has been largely descriptive – questioning in many cases whether communities exist in contemporary societies, given the buffeting of capitalism, industrialisation and urbanisation. The success of network analysis in discovering communities under these circumstances has shifted the focus away from simply documenting the continued existence of communities to demonstrating how large-scale structural patterns affect the ways in which specific community structures contribute to social production and reproduction. (Wellman and Berkowitz 1988: 8)

Wellman applies a similar approach to the study of community in the Internet age. What counts, he argues, is not the physical proximity of the individual members of a community but rather the types of social ties (weak/detached or strong/intimate) and support networks that might be found either on- or offline (see also Rheingold 1993). In a paper with Milena Gulia, Wellman offers the following provocation: 'Social network analysts have had to educate traditional, place-oriented, community sociologists that community can stretch well beyond the neighbourhood' (1999: 169). Nevertheless, Wellman and Gulia initially appear to arrive at a similar conclusion to that of Castells: that 'weak ties flourish online' (ibid.: 178). In a later text with Caroline Haythornthwaite, however, Wellman argues that 'even before the advent of the Internet, there has been a move from all encompassing, socially controlling communities to individualized, fragmented personal communities' (2002: 32). This statement implies that community is not declining in 'network society', as Castells suggests, but rather changing in form. Things are, in fact, more complex than this, for first, as Wellman and Gulia observe, just because individualized relations might flourish online, the Internet does not necessarily work 'against the maintenance of socially close, strong ties' (1999: 178), especially among specialized support groups. Second, in line with the basic principles of social network analysis, virtual communities are not to be treated in isolation from the topology of networked society more broadly, for 'despite all the talk about virtual community transcending time and space *sui generis*, much contact is between people who see each other in person and live locally' (Wellman Gulia 1999: 179).

In sum, social network analysis is less concerned with the technological structures of networks in themselves than with the human connections between nodes (at various scales) that make networks possible. In this view, social networks are about the human connections made through new media rather than the protocols, hardware and informational flows of new media infrastructures that lie at the centre of other, more techno-centric approaches (see for instance Kittler 1999, or Manovich

2001; see also **Chapters 4** and **7**). The key feature of social network analysis is that it focuses upon the 'patterns of relations between and among people' (Garton et al. 1999: 76), and for this reason declares that when 'a computer network connects people or organizations, it is a social network' (Garton et al.: 75). In other words, new media networks are not of interest per se unless they open the possibility of new connectivities between human actors – at which point they are said to become *social* in form. Garton et al. explain: 'just as a computer network is a set of machines connected by a set of cables, a social network is a set of people (or organizations or other social entities) connected by a set of social relations, such as friendship, co-working, or information exchange' (Garton et al. 1999).

A parallel is thus drawn between computer networks and social networks on the grounds that they share a similar infrastructure defined by the connections of which it is made up rather than by a bounded territorial whole (such as a network society). The task of social network analysis is to plot and interpret these connections by using the concept of network as a *representational* tool rather than as a theoretical metaphor. This approach is thus quite different to that forwarded by Castells. What is striking about this position is that little attention is paid in this account to the ways in which technology might shape the social relations to which it gives rise, or of how networks are made up not simply of humans but of complex relations between a range of human and non-human entities. The idea of social network analysis is that computer networks become social when they connect individuals, groups and institutions in various ways, and for this reason it is the human or the social that is the primary object of study. But what this approach perhaps misses is the ways in which such networks, especially today, make these connections possible, and the ways in which social networks are structured by various technologies as a consequence. Social network analysis uses the idea of a network to represent or plot new forms of human connectivity, but tends to leave aside the range of social and/or technological forces that make these forms possible, and which perhaps influence the various topologies that they take.

ACTOR NETWORK THEORY

This question of the connection between the technological and the social, along with human and non-human connectivity, lies at the centre of a different body of work that has become known as actor network theory (or ANT). Actor network theory has been highly influential in opening new ways for thinking about questions of mobility and connectivity (see for example John Urry's writings on global mobilities (2000, 2003)), while at the same time, paradoxically, retaining a deep ambivalence toward the concept of network. One of the clearest expressions of this approach is to be found in the collection *Actor Network Theory and After*, edited by John Law and John Hassard (1999). Law opens this collection with a summary of the main aims, achievements and difficulties of actor network theory to date. He says that there are two main aspects to this approach. The first is an emphasis on what he calls the 'semiotics of materiality' or 'relational materiality'. This is the idea that the relationality of signs is to be lifted from the realm of semiotics and extended to the analysis of material forms, such as common everyday objects. This is something quite different to Social Network Analysis. Law explains: 'It [ANT] takes the semiotic insight, that of the relationality of entities, the notion that they are produced in relations, and applies this ruthlessly to all the materials – and not simply to those that are linguistic' (Law 1999: 4). As we will see in **Chapter 3**, such an approach is central also to the work of Donna Haraway (1997), who addresses the connection between the material and the semiotic through the study of entities that are both material forms and signifiers of a new regime of intellectual property (for example, the Flavr Savr tomato). Law, however, talks of a second main aspect to actor network theory: an interest in performativity. This concerns the question of how entities (human or non-human) become what they are through their connection to other entities (something Manuel DeLanda (2006) has recently addressed through a focus on different 'assemblages'). What intrigues Law is 'How it is that things get per-formed (and perform themselves) into relations that are relatively stable and stay in place' (Law 1999: 4).

Law answers this question by forging a notion of network as 'an alternative topo-logical system' in which 'elements retain their spatial integrity *by virtue of their position in a set of links or relations*' (Law 1999: 6). He argues that there are two main ways of dealing with the concept of network. The first is 'to insist, robustly, that the term is indeed relatively neutral, a descriptive vocabulary which makes possible the analysis of different patterns of connection which embody or represent different topological possibilities' (Law 1999: 7). This position is similar to that forwarded by social network analysis, and is one that Law attempts to move away from in favour of a second, more critical view. This is that 'the notion of the network is itself a form – or perhaps a family of forms – of spatiality: that it imposes strong restrictions on the conditions of topological possibility. And that, accordingly, it tends to limit and homogenize the character of links, the character of possible relations, and so the character of possible entities' (Law 1999). The problem, for Law is that the concept of network does not have enough analytical purchase because it is also already a form, one that treats all entities within its reach as being connectable and therefore similar in some way. Law objects to this approach because it does not tell us enough about how links are made within and between networks, and by extension *how* entities become what they are. His response is to move beyond the idea of 'a network' to insist instead on the basic heterogeneity of (difference between) entities, along with a renewed emphasis of the *complexity* of relations through which these are formed.

Bruno Latour, in an essay in Law and Hassard, is more aggressive in his attack on the concept of 'network' and on the idea of actor-network theory more generally. He declares that 'there are four things that do not work with actor-network theory: the word actor, the word network, the word theory and the hyphen!' (Latour 1999: 15). He starts with the concept that is of interest to us here:

> The first nail in the coffin is I guess the word 'network' … This is the great danger of using a technical metaphor slightly ahead of everyone's common use. Now that the World Wide Web exists, everyone believes they understand what a network is. While twenty years ago there was still some freshness in the term as a critical tool against notions as diverse as institution, society, nation-state and, more generally, any flat surface, it has lost any cutting edge … 'Down with rigid institutions', they all say, 'long live flexible networks'. (Latour 1999: 15)

It is worth pausing for a moment to reflect on some of the key points forwarded in this passage (some of which Latour later retracts, as we shall see below). First, Latour argues that while early metaphors of 'network' had some degree of critical purchase, today the term has become synonymous with attempts to bypass analysis of institutional forms or structures in favour of the study of flexibility and flows. For Latour, this neglect of the question of topology is a mistake, as potentially it leaves institutional forms immune to analysis. Second, Latour hints that the widespread usage of the metaphor 'network' in the social sciences is worrying because networks are technical forms that are more sophisticated than are commonly thought. It is here worth recalling from the opening section of this chapter that contrary to most sociological usages of the term, networks can take many different forms and can be open and closed to varying degrees. For this reason, it would be wrong to think of a network simply as a decentred, 'non-linear grid of multiple connections' (van Loon 2006: 307) because in practice networks can assume a range of different topologies, some of which are distinctly hierarchical in form. This means, for Latour, that the idea of network is never something which can be simply given or presupposed.

Perhaps surprisingly, at this point, Latour finds merit in Deleuze and Guattari's idea of the rhizome (a complex system of roots that branch out and connect to each other horizontally) which, he says, formulates a conception of the network as something that is always transforming itself through emergent connections between different entities. The importance of the rhizome is that it depicts a system characterized by connections rather than by clearly defined borders or territorial closure.

Deleuze and Guattari argue that the rhizome is defined by 'principles of connection and heterogeneity: any point of a rhizome can be connected to anything other, and must be' (1987: 7). In this view, networks are dynamic systems that contain endless creative possibilities, for they bring entities into contact in ways that would previously have been unthinkable, while at the same time defying closure within any predefined intellectual or geographical territory. Latour's interest in this is how entities are formed and transformed once they become connected to each other. He complains that it is exactly this focus that is lost in recent metaphors of 'the network'. In a damning passage, he declares that

> [with] the new popularisation of the word network, it now means transport *without* deformation, an instantaneous, unmediated access to every piece of information. That is exactly the opposite of what we meant. What I would like to call 'double click information' has killed the last bit of the critical cutting edge of the notion of network. I don't think we should use it anymore at least not to mean the type of transformations and translations we now want to explore. (Latour 1999: 15–16)

In this respect, Latour shares similar ground with John Law. What interests him are the connections or associations that make networks possible, along with the ways in which entities are transformed once they become associated with each other. For Latour, attention to such detail threatens to be lost in an online world in which connections are instantly and routinely forged through the hyperlinking of objects and information. Again like Law, the important point for Latour is to consider the actual operation of networks in connecting together different entities, leading him to suggest replacing the concept of the network with the reverse: the *work-net* (see Latour in Gane 2004: 83). Recently, however, Latour has returned to the idea of the network: 'I still think it is useful. I have changed my mind … because now I am using the work of Gabriel Tarde' (Latour in Gane 2004: 2). This reference to Tarde returns us to the writings of Deleuze and Guattari, in particular *A Thousand Plateaus* (1987) where Deleuze and Guattari pay homage to Tarde (1843–1904) for giving attention to 'the world of detail, or of the infinitesimal: the little *imitations, oppositions*, and *inventions* constituting an entire realm of subrepresentative matter' (1987: 218–19). What is important here is the marking out of different types of *flow* (of 'belief and desire'): '*Imitation is the propagation of a flow; opposition is binarization, the making binary of flows; invention is a conjugation or connection of different flows*' (Deleuze and Guattari 1987: 219). Latour (2002) also pays homage to the work of Tarde, but for slightly different reasons. Like Deleuze and Guattari, Latour is attracted to analysis of 'the world of detail, or of the infinitesimal' – that world of everyday entities and objects that are formed and transformed through their relations with one another.

But beyond this, Latour seeks to develop Tarde's idea of the social, which, he argues, is framed by a theory of *association* rather than an overarching vision of 'society'. He explains: 'there were already at the origin of sociology, at least in France, two traditions. One of them saw the social as a special part of reality ... and another one saw very well that what counts in the social is the type of connections that are made' (Latour in Gane 2004: 82). Latour places Tarde and himself in this latter tradition, and in this context argues that the word network is still useful insofar as it orients sociology toward the analysis of connections and associations between different actors and entities.

This, for Latour is where the value of actor network theory really lies: in the 'tracing of associations' so that they render 'the movement of the social visible to the reader' (Latour 2005: 128). What is important, Latour argues, is not to see the social in terms of a screen onto which all actors and entities can be projected, but rather to see it in terms of complex and dynamic connections that need analytic work and a close attention to detail in order to be analysed and understood. In this view, actors are not passive entities that can be explained away through grand societal forces but need to be observed and analysed in their own right. Hence, Latour states that a 'good ANT account is a narrative or a description or a proposition where all the actors do something and don't just sit there' (1999). 'Network' is not a description of something that is simply out there, but rather a set of connections that have to be actively made. Latour concludes: 'What is important in the word network is the word *work*. You need work in order to make the connection' (Latour in Gane 2004: 83). Such work, in Latour's view, is today the vocation of the sociologist.

CONCLUSION

This chapter has opened up four different approaches to and uses of the concept of network. The first of these came from computer science and focuses on the technical infrastructures that make communication between different new media devices possible. The basic idea to be taken from this section is that networks have different architectures or topologies, and are only able to work if suitable standards or protocols are in place to ensure smooth cross-platform communication. The second approach – that of Manuel Castells – uses network as a metaphor for a new type of capitalist society which is more flexible, decentred and individualized than previous forms. The third approach, social network analysis, uses the idea of network as a representational form to help plot emergent forms of connectivity between humans at various scales (both individual and collective). The emphasis in this approach is on the ways in which computer networks become social rather than technological forms as soon as they connect people or organizations together. Finally, actor network theory looks at connections between humans and non-human entities. This theory insists that 'network' should never be used in the social sciences simply as a descriptive form, for the role of such sciences is to *make* such connections between entities, and with this analyse what makes these possible along with the effects they might bring.

This leaves us with a difficult question: should a concept such as network be employed as a descriptive or methodological tool (as in the case of Castells and perhaps social network analysis) or instead be used to pose problems and make connections between entities as part of an active programme of research? Knox et al. sense that Latour's unease with the concept of network lies with 'people taking the metaphor of the network as a truism', or when such concepts are used as 'descriptors of structures rather than heuristic devices' (Knox et al. 2006: 133). This is precisely Latour's complaint: 'Network is a concept, not a thing out there. It is a tool to help describe something, not what is being described ...' (Latour 2005: 131). In this reading, it does not matter whether the concept or metaphor of network is close to its material realization just as long as this concept remains useful and is not mistaken for a description in itself. For Latour, the right way to think about network is as a concept that helps social scientists make connections or associations between different components or 'assemblages' (see also DeLanda 2006), be these animal, human or machine. But in practice things are more complex than this because it is difficult to separate out network as a concept from network as a description of a material formation. One reason for this is that analyses of social and cultural phenomena in terms of networks evoke a metaphor that comes from technical origins. Indeed, it is difficult to think of networks without recalling images of wires, cables, telegraphs and circuits, or indeed to think outside of the media networks through which we express and communicate our thoughts (see Idhe 1979: 98). This means that the concept of network, especially if it is to remain useful, can never be divorced completely from its existence as a material form, otherwise what could this concept possibly mean? The irony is that where sociologists and media theorists have tried to remain faithful to these technical origins they have, for the most part, adopted a single vision of a network as a paradigmatic form: that it is a complex, non-linear, decentred, and emergent property. This is somewhat apparent in the work of Castells, and more so in Deleuze-inspired approaches (see also Urry 2003 and Lash 2002). The problem this brings is that the hierarchical structures, rules and protocols of networks have perhaps not received as much attention as they should (Alex Galloway 2004, 2006 is a notable exception), at least within the social sciences. In our view this is a mistake, as questions of power, access and control within networks, both social and technological, are clearly just as important as ever (see Graham and Marvin 2001).

The basic question underpinning this chapter is of the work for which the concept 'network' might be employed. John Urry has suggested that in Castells' work the 'global remains rather taken for granted and there is not the range of theoretical terms necessary to analyse the emergent properties of the networked "global" level' (Urry 2003: 11). For Urry, the problem is that the term 'network' is expected to do too much theoretical work in his argument (Urry 2003), not least because 'almost all phenomena are seen through the single and undifferentiated prism of "network"'. Urry's complaint is, first, that the term network is often used too loosely, and, as Latour suggests, is presented as being self-evident rather than as something to be explained – especially as networks themselves may take many different physical and relational forms. But alongside this there is a second issue: that the concept of network is not enough on its own to promote a deep understanding of the new media age. This concept is clearly useful in the social sciences as it provides opportunities for constructing dynamic images of the connections people make and the bonds that they form, and also provides opportunities for compiling data about these connections. But for this concept not to be overloaded it must belong to a wider network of concepts that are useful for the analysis of the manifold intricacies of contemporary society and culture, such as: information, interface, simulation, interactivity and archive. It is to the concept of information that we turn next.

Chapter Summary

■ From the mid-1990s onward new concepts and metaphors of 'network' have passed from computer science into social theory and media studies.

■ Networks are often thought of as being decentred in form, but in practice they are highly structured and are governed by a range of different protocols.

■ The concept of network can be used to think about the changing structures and dynamics of contemporary capitalist society (Castells).

■ It is possible to theorize social structures in terms of relationality or connectivity (social network analysis).

■ Attention also needs to be paid to the ways through which connections are forged between humans, technologies and objects (actor network theory).

3 INFORMATION

> It is conceivable that the nation-states will one day fight for control of information, just as they battled in the past for control over territory, and afterwards for control of access to and exploitation of raw materials and cheap labour.
>
> Lyotard (1984: 5)

It is widely claimed today that we live in an information or 'informational' society (see for example Bell 1976, Castells 1996, Mattelart 2003). The argument behind this claim is that information is becoming a – or perhaps even *the* – major commodity for exchange in advanced capitalist societies, and because of this previous forms of industrialism are giving way to 'informationalism': a new mode of life which 'is oriented toward technological development, that is toward the accumulation of knowledge and toward high levels of complexity in information processing' (Castells 1996: 17). There has been extensive debate across the social sciences about the impact and global reach of this claimed shift toward post-industrial society but, by contrast, surprisingly little attention has been paid to the basic concept that underpins this debate: *information*. This chapter will attempt to fill this gap by examining the workings of this concept in a range of different disciplinary settings. The chapter will open with a consideration of the early information science of Claude Shannon and Warren Weaver, and will look at how this science has been reworked by media theorists such as Marshall McLuhan and, more recently, Friedrich Kittler. Following this, arguments about the materiality or embodied nature of information will be addressed by analysing the writings of Donna Haraway and, briefly, Katherine N. Hayles on the related idea of *informatics*. Finally, we will turn to analysis of the 'information society' (Manuel Castells), and to more radical theories of the commodification of information (Jean-François Lyotard) and information critique (Scott Lash). It will be argued, however, that no single concept of information forwarded by any of the above theorists is on its own sufficient. For on one hand, definitions of information from within information science and cybernetics tend to work in abstraction from a theory of capitalist society and culture, while on the other, the information society literature tends to lack a clear-cut definition of what information actually is, along with a technical understanding of how it is produced and engineered. By way of conclusion, we suggest working beyond this current impasse between sociological and engineering approaches to the study of information in order to produce a critical yet technically informed theory of information society.

INFORMATION SCIENCE

A useful starting point for thinking about the concept of information is Claude Shannon's 1948 essay 'The Mathematical Theory of Communication' (Shannon and Weaver 1949). For students of the social and cultural sciences it might seem odd to open a chapter on information through consideration of a work that is overtly mathematical in orientation, but the significance of this essay – which some have called '*the* foundational text for information theory' (Johnston 1997: 6) – should not be understated, not least because today, nearly sixty years after it was first published, it continues to influence work at the cutting edge of media and cultural theory (Hayles 1999, Kittler 1992; see Gane 2005a). To understand why, one must focus on the basic philosophical argument that is forwarded throughout the course of this text. This argument is that the technical problem of *how* communication takes place should, in the first instance, be separated out from and prioritized over sociological or philosophical questions concerning the *meaning* of communication. This is because Shannon – who was an employee of the Bell Telephone Company at the time of writing this text – conceives of communication as an engineering problem. Shannon argues that engineers of communication systems are confronted by a basic challenge – namely, how a communication system is to process particular messages when these are unknown at the time of the system's design. To use a present-day example, how can a mobile phone transmit text messages that are chosen by a user but that are not known in advance by the designer of the phone? Shannon's answer is to conceive of messages as choices from a pre-defined set of variables, and, in line with this, to view communication as a question of probability rather than of semantics. This means that he explains communication in mathematical – or rather, statistical – terms. His basic idea is that a *measure* of information, along with a rate of production and transmission, is produced when a particular message is chosen from a set of possible variables. This might at first seem to be a complex approach, but the underlying idea is in fact straightforward. To again use the example of the mobile phone: in order for a text message to be composed and sent, the system handling the message must be able to recognize and code the characters the user selects, even if the precise text of the message typed is not known in advance. For such a system to work, it must be designed to process combinations of variables from a given set, and this is made easier because the probability of a user choosing certain characters to form a particular message can be calculated as a statistical measure. This means, in turn, that communication can be explained in mathematical terms. For Shannon, the basic rule of such work is as follows: the more complex a messaging system is, the greater the choice of possible characters it offers (for example from a phone keypad), and hence the higher the rate of information, as a *statistical measure*, that such a system can generate and handle.

The main feature of this approach is that from the point of view of designing and engineering communications systems, the question of how information is created and transmitted is more important than what information in itself might mean. By extension, the physical design of a communication system, for Shannon, structures the meaning and content of the information that passes through it. This idea will be addressed in detail below, but first there is a further step to Shannon's argument that needs to be considered. Shannon assigns the basic components – or what he calls the 'physical counterparts' – of communication systems a mathematical function. In his view, there are five main components of all such systems: the information source, the transmitter, the channel, the receiver and the destination. This five-stage model has since been reworked by theorists as far removed as Jacques Lacan (1988) and Umberto Eco (1989), but it is worth returning to Shannon's original writings to look at the function he ascribes to each individual component within this model.

The first component, the information source, is simply that entity, human or machine, which produces the message or sequence of messages that is to be communicated. The transmitter (the second component) then operates on or *encodes* the message so that it can be passed through the physical channel or medium of communication in the form of a signal. Shannon explains: 'In telephony this operation consists merely of changing sound pressure into a proportional electrical current. In telegraphy we have an encoding operation which produces a sequence of dots, dashes and spaces on the channel corresponding to the message' (Shannon and Weaver 1949: 33). This signal then passes through the channel (the third component), which is 'merely the medium used to transmit the signal from transmitter to receiver' (Shannon and Weaver 1949). During the course of this process of transmission, however, the signal risks modification by unwanted sources of *noise*, which means in turn that 'the received signal is not necessarily the same as that sent out by the transmitter' (Shannon and Weaver 1949: 65). This process of distortion complicates things greatly. For as one might expect, noise in the signal chain decreases the accuracy of a transmitted signal and in so doing introduces a degree of loss into the system. The flip side of this, however, is something unexpected: that noise, because it expands the limits of a set of messages, increases the range of information a system might contain. Paradoxically, then, a decrease in the accuracy of the representation of a given message may well mean more in terms of information, for it brings an accompanying increase in the range of possible forms this message may take. This only makes sense if information is treated, as Shannon suggests, as a statistical measure rather than as a body of ideas that has its own integral importance and meaning. Warren Weaver explains this position in relation to the idea of noise: 'It is generally true that when there is noise, the received signal exhibits greater information – or better, the received signal is selected out of a more varied set than is the transmitted signal' (Shannon and Weaver 1949: 19). This leads, in turn, to the fourth component of the communication system – the receiver – which reconstructs or *decodes* the message from the signal so that it can arrive at its destination (the fifth component), even if, as Shannon observes, the message fails to arrive precisely as intended.

Warren Weaver – in an accompanying essay to the 'Mathematical Theory of Communication' – illustrates the basis of Shannon's argument by separating out three quite different levels of analysis for the study of communication. The first of these (what Weaver calls 'level A') deals with the technical problem of communica- tion, and asks 'how accurately can the symbols of communication be transmitted?' (Shannon and Weaver 1949: 4). The second level ('level B') concerns questions of semantics, and addresses in particular the question of 'how precisely do the transmitted symbols [of a message] convey the desired meaning?' (Shannon and Weaver 1949). The third level ('level C') is more sociological in orientation, and asks 'how effectively does the received meaning affect conduct in the desired way?' (Shannon and Weaver 1949). The basic argument of both Shannon and Weaver is that the technical problem of communication (level A) is to be given primacy over both questions of meaning (B) and action (C), for while the semantic aspects of information are irrelevant to communication as a technical problem, the accuracy with which individual messages can be transmitted and received directly influences both the meaning of these messages and their capacity to be 'affective'. In sum, this means that 'signal accuracies' at level A directly condition the possibility of both semantics (B) and the sphere of action (C), but not vice versa. Weaver explains: 'any limitations discovered in the theory at level A necessarily apply to levels B and C' and, as a consequence, 'the theory of level A is, at least to a significant degree, a theory of levels B and C' (Shannon and Weaver 1949: 6). The technological form of transmission, which includes the coding of messages into signals, the physical channel through which messages flow, and the potential for noise to impact upon and distort these messages, is thus taken to be the primary object of study. This means that Shannon and Weaver start with the analysis of the mathematics and engineering of communication and relegate questions of meaning and social action to second- and third-order problems – a position which, even today, reverses the priorities of mainstream sociological and philosophical approaches to communication and information, which tend to bypass level A in favour of analysis of levels B and C.

Shannon's theory of information might seem dry and overly technical at first sight, but it comes alive when considered through the lens of writings by media theorists such as Marshall McLuhan and Friedrich Kittler (see also **Chapter 7**). If one looks, for example, at the underlying argument of McLuhan's (1964) key work *Understanding Media*, it is clear that a theory of information is present that draws implicitly from the work of Shannon and Weaver. McLuhan's position in this book pays no attention to their call for a mathematics of information, but nevertheless follows the main thrust of their argument by prioritizing analysis of the technology of message transmission over interpretation of its content, hence his famous declaration that the 'medium is the message'. For Shannon and Weaver there is, in fact, no real message but only a signal (see Hayles 1999: 18), and it is the ability to code and decode this signal through mathematical operations that, for them, is of primary interest. McLuhan, however, extends the basic logic of their argument by asserting that it is the channel or technology of communication that shapes the content transmitted rather than vice versa. This is why, for McLuhan, the *medium* is the message, for information – which is now something that has a materiality and a content and hence is more than just a statistical measure – can never be understood in isolation from the technological devices through which it is produced and communicated. The power of technology to shape its content is a constant source of fascination for McLuhan, who parodied the 'mosaic' form of television culture (fast-moving images and short sound-bytes of information) in later books such as *The Medium is the Massage* (McLuhan and Fiore 1967). But beyond this, McLuhan gives Shannon and Weaver's communication system a further twist, for the information source (the sender) and final destination of communication disappear from his account. McLuhan focuses instead on the changes that communication technologies introduce in general into 'human affairs', and this leads in turn to a position that wavers between a basic humanism (placing 'Man' at the centre of all things) and an alternative stance in which human subjectivity disappears into the machinery of communication. This tension subsequently remains unresolved throughout McLuhan's writings, for on one hand media are seen to be 'extensions of man' (1964: 3), while on the other they are said to 'work us over completely' (1967: 26).

Friedrich Kittler (who openly acknowledges his debt to Shannon – see for example 1992: 67) pounces on such slippages in McLuhan's work. First off, Kittler declares that 'Media determine our situation, which – in spite or because of it – deserves a description' (1999: xxxix). This is a strong statement: media *determine* our situation, and because of this they must be subjected to critical analysis. Kittler warns, however, that such analysis is not likely to be easy for at least three reasons.

First, since the majority of media technologies have military origins (as also argued by Virilio 1998), their historical details remain, in many cases, classified and thus inaccessible, meaning that there exists a marked distance between what Kittler calls 'files and facts'. Second, media can only be described and analysed through the use of other media (Kittler 1996), which in turn means that it is difficult to gain critical distance from the very technologies that are being placed into question. And third, information generated by new media technologies and which allows us to analyse their workings increasingly takes the form of binary code, which not only possesses little meaning in itself but is designed to be processed by machines. For this reason, Kittler, like Shannon, proposes that information, and more generally its medium of communication, cannot be 'understood' in an interpretive sense. Kittler (1986: 166) here argues that McLuhan's project of 'understanding media' is based on an 'anthropocentric illusion' (a misguided projection of humanness onto technologies and machines). This is because meaning is not intrinsic or prior to technology but rather made possible and directed by its presence: 'the dominant information technologies of the day control all understanding and its illusions' (Kittler 1999: xl). For this reason, Kittler seeks not to understand media as such – for what could a technology such as a mobile phone in itself possibly mean? – but rather to document the historical conditions of their emergence, along with the structures of communication and understanding they subsequently make possible – what Kittler calls a technical *a priori*. This 'post-hermeneutic' approach (Wellberry 1990: vii–xvi), which again is in complete accordance with that proposed by Shannon and Weaver, seeks to open a 'semantics-free space' (Kittler 1992: 67) in which description and analysis of technological forms is seen to come before and then, in turn, to structure interpretive questions of meaning and action (Weaver's levels B and C).

Kittler, however, goes further than this, and moves beyond Shannon and Weaver by formulating an approach that he calls 'information materialism', which looks at the ways in which information and communication systems are increasingly merging into one: information is 'transformed into matter and matter into information' (Kittler 1997: 126). One of the key aspects of this approach is that it attempts to reverse the sociological preoccupation with the human subject and human agency by starting instead with an analysis of media (something we will explore in **Chapter 7** in our analysis of the 'posthuman'). Kittler proclaims, for example, that 'what remains of people is what media can store and communicate. What counts are not the messages or the content with which they equip so-called souls for the duration of a technological era, but rather (and in strict accordance with McLuhan) their circuits, the very schematism of perceptibility' (Kittler 1999: xl–xli). Kittler and McLuhan here reach a point of convergence: the primary focus of media theory is to be the material structures of communication technologies and the changes these introduce into culture, not the ways in which such technologies are *used* or the content of the messages or information that pass through them. But for Kittler, this means pushing McLuhan's study of media into the digital age so that computers, their storage capacities, and their networks are placed at the centre of analysis. It also means extending Shannon's communication system – made up of information source, the transmitter, the channel, the receiver and the destination (which mutate in Kittler's reading into 'the source, sender, channel, receiver and drain of streams of information' (1990: 370), so that the destination disappears) – by looking at media in terms of their capacity for information *storage*. And this emphasis on storage or technologized *memory* is a point of departure away from Shannon and Weaver, for no longer is information treated purely as a probability function, but rather as a material property that is in no way distinct from the physical components that make it – or the choice between different variables – possible.

INFORMATION AND INFORMATICS

The materiality of information has also been called into question in a quite different way by recent feminist thinkers such as Donna Haraway and Katherine N. Hayles. Both Haraway and Hayles are deeply influenced by the early information science of Claude Shannon, but argue that its analysis of the material underpinnings of communication goes not nearly far enough. For although Shannon breaks down communication into five physical components, each of these is subsequently assigned a mathematical function and, in line with this, information is treated as a statistical measure rather than as a material form. This is something that Katherine Hayles objects to, for she argues that such thinking divorces information from its body, and in so doing neglects to explain its instantiation within various media – a move that she has recently called 'the dream of information' (Hayles 2005a: 62). This same accusation cannot be levelled at McLuhan, whose primary interest is the way in which different media produce, package and communicate information, along with the impact these processes have on 'human affairs'. McLuhan, by extension, analyses the connection of various media to the human body, and famously defines media 'as extensions of some human faculty – psychic or physical' (1967: 26). But, nevertheless, there are limitations to his account. Perhaps the most obvious of these is that while he talks of the shaping of information by different media he says little directly about the connection of information either to the human body or to the capitalist marketplace. These same criticisms might also be levelled at Friedrich Kittler, who shows little interest in either the human body per se or the dynamics of contemporary capitalist culture. To address these issues, we will look first at the writings of Haraway and Hayles on information and informatics, before turning to theories of 'informational' capitalism in the final section of this chapter.

At the centre of Haraway's now famous 'Cyborg Manifesto' (1991: 149–81) is a consideration of the intricate and complex connections between information, power and the body. One of Haraway's chief aims in this essay is to move away from an analysis of power as a purely hierarchal form, and to formulate instead an 'informatics of domination' that centres on the 'scary new networks' of the digital age. For Haraway, a key feature of the contemporary world is the emergence of new decentred forms of power that reside in networks of intelligent information systems, and which extend themselves from work into leisure and play. Power, she argues, is now just as likely to reside in information systems (the primary one today being the Internet), as it is in physical relations of production (as viewed, for example, by Marx), and for this reason Haraway talks of an *informatics* of domination. This conception of informatics revisits the information science and cybernetic theory of Shannon and Weaver to suggest that nothing, in essence, can resist being coded as information, including the 'human' body. In Haraway's words: 'No objects, spaces, or bodies are sacred in themselves; any component can be interfaced with any other if the proper standard, the proper code, can be constructed for processing signals in a common language' (Haraway 1991: 163). Haraway's answer is to bring together information science and biology and in so doing to translate '*the world into a problem of coding*' (Haraway 1991: 164; emphasis in original). This move, in turn, raises many pressing questions, including: what happens when genetic information or source codes can be manipulated and interfaced to produce new forms of exchange and kinship between previously discrete entities, whether these are human, animal or machine? For if the right code can be found, seemingly closed systems can interface with one another, giving rise to the possibility of new, seemingly 'transversal' or boundaryless forms of life and culture. An example of such a form is the Flavr Savr tomato, which incorporates a gene from a deep-sea flounder so that it decays at a slower rate. Haraway (1997: 56) labels this tomato a 'transgenetic organism' as it is a genetically modified life-form that transgresses previous species boundaries. But how are we to make sense of such entities, and of the emergence more generally of what Haraway calls cyborgs: organisms that are not purely human, animal or machine, and which cross and confuse more boundaries than they uphold?

Information is a key concept in Haraway's understanding and vision of this new world. Her argument is that traditional divisions between nature and culture are losing their meaning, for both domains are giving way to an array of complex and often interchangeable codes that are bringing together previously unconnected life forms and technologies. This possibility of common languages or codes – most notably genetic codes – places all life forms (organic and technological) into what

Haraway calls a 'field of difference': a field in which seemingly heterogeneous entities become interfaceable because they share an underlying structural sameness. Haraway develops this position through a dialogue with the early cybernetic theory of Norbert Wiener and the information science of Shannon and Weaver. In her terms, information is the new instrument of translation that effaces natural and cultural boundaries by reducing all elements to a comparable code (for example, the genetic code of the Flavr Savr tomato). She declares that 'The world is subdivided by boundaries differentially permeable to information. Information is just that kind of quantifiable (unit, basis of unity) which allows universal translation, and so unhindered instrumental power (called effective communication)' (Haraway 1991: 164). In Shannon and Weaver's mathematical theory of communication, as discussed above, some degree of system closure (in the form of a 'general set') is required in order for a statistical measure of information to be produced. Haraway, in turn, applies this theory to the study of the human body: 'Human beings, like any other component or subsystem, must be localised in a system architecture whose basic modes of operation are probabilistic' (1991: 163). But she also goes beyond Shannon and Weaver by arguing that as systems interface and cross into each other, new forms of meta-information emerge that work across previous system boundaries. This is especially the case when boundaries between different types of organic and non-organic beings start to fade as they become hybridized and give rise to new 'biotic components, i.e. special kinds of information-processing devices' (Haraway 1991: 164). At this point, biological science starts to merge with information science and cybernetics to become a form of 'cryptography' that proceeds through the decoding of information patterns or genomes. (For example, in August 2005, geneticists finally decoded the DNA of the chimpanzee.) Code – or rather, *information* – is the key to this situation, and as a form it is itself transversal in basis: it is neither simply biological nor simply cultural in basis but an interface between, and perhaps a confusion of, the two.

Information, then, for Haraway, is not simply a probability function (as it is for Shannon and Weaver) but a *code* that is entwined within the physical structures of technological media and bodily systems. As stated above, Haraway sees information as bringing the possibility of a culture of 'universal translation' through the inter-facing of previously discrete system codes. But she argues at the same time that such a development brings the threat of a new 'instrumental power'. Haraway here shifts Foucault's analysis of power/knowledge to a concern for power/information (something we return to in the conclusion to **Chapter 5**), or what she calls 'techno-biopower'. (For a reflection on this see Gane and Haraway 2006.) The danger, for Haraway, is that as information becomes the metalanguage that can open out and fuse seemingly closed systems through the reduction of all life to a single (genetic) code, otherness – that which is singular and which has traditionally defied translation and incorporation within any system – is placed increasingly under threat. This position is similar to that of Jean Baudrillard, who warns that the tranversality (boundarylessness) of contemporary capitalist culture gives rise to the 'hell of the same', a condition whereby otherness is coded as difference – as something that can be qualified, quantified, and potentially exchanged as something that possesses 'value'. For Haraway, similarly, the apparent heterogeneity of contemporary culture is underpinned by a basic homogeneity at the underlying level of information or code. In the face of this, again like Baudrillard, she sees value in phenomena that defy the possibility of such translation. She argues, for example, that while the translation of all bodies and culture into a universal code carries the threat of an 'unhindered instrumental power', there are accompanying possibilities of resistance that rest on the disruption of communication between different systems, and which therefore threaten to spoil the coding of life into information. She declares: 'The biggest threat to … [instrumental] power is interruption of communication' (Haraway 1991: 164). And adds: 'Cyborg politics is the struggle for language and the struggle against perfect communication, against the one code that translates all meaning perfectly, the central dogma of phallogocentrism' (p. 176). In these terms, noise – that key term for Shannon and Weaver – might be employed to serve a political purpose.

Katherine Hayles in many ways builds on Haraway's position (see Hayles 2006). We will look in detail at Hayles's work in our consideration of simulation and the posthuman in **Chapter 7**, but here it is worth observing that in line with Haraway, Hayles questions the liberal presuppositions that underpin early information theory and cybernetics, along with the assumption that information can be abstracted from all underlying material contexts, conditions and practices. In her key work *How We Became Posthuman*, Hayles argues that information cannot be thought of outside of its connection with matter, for it is always *embodied* in some way. In so doing, she calls into question 'posthuman' separations of information from matter, and mind from body. This emphasis on the human body places Hayles in opposition to Kittler (see above), for whom machines and mathematics are more important: 'What remains of people is what media can store and communicate' (Kittler 1999: xl–xli). Against this view, Hayles insists that media are to be thought of in connection to the bodily practices through which information is brought into the material world. Like Haraway, Hayles argues that the concept of informatics is central to this project. She defines informatics as

> the material, technological, economic, and social structures that make the
> information age possible. Informatics includes the following: the late capitalist
> mode of flexible accumulation; the hardware and software that have merged

telecommunications with computer technology; the patterns of living that emerge from and depend on access to large data banks and instantaneous transmission of messages; and the physical habits – of posture, eye focus, hand motions, and neural connections – that are reconfiguring the human body in conjunction with information technologies. (Hayles 1999: 313)

In sum, informatics refers to the inseparability of information from a range of material settings and practices. In the above passage, there are four main axes along which analysis of information is to be pursued: first, its connection to the emergence of new forms of capitalist finance and culture; second, the interplay between hardware and software in making networked flows of information possible; third, the emergence of forms of instant living that are tied to the acceleration of information access and exchange; and finally, the connection of information to the human body and lived space. Oddly, Hayles's own account is confined mainly to an analysis of the second and the final of points of this list, in particular to the study of the connection of hardware/body and mind/software in the production of consciousness (see Hayles 2005b), and the embodiment of information within different media (with little, if any, consideration of lived spaces or urban settings). Hayles's account, then, while making a strong case for the embodiment or materiality of information, is one-sided, not least because it fails to look in any detail at the dynamics of capitalist culture that are driving the acceleration of information production, exchange and consumption. Haraway (1997: 1–22) touches on such dynamics in her analysis of the commodification of transgenetic elements such as the Flavr Savr tomato through the emergence of new forms of intellectual property, along with a new syntax of ownership which includes the copyright© and trademark™. But for a broader analysis of information as part of capitalist culture it is necessary to look elsewhere, namely to sociological studies of information society and informational capitalism.

INFORMATION SOCIETY AND CRITIQUE

As stated in the introduction to this chapter, the idea of an 'information society' is now commonplace in the social sciences. In simple terms, such a society centres upon the production, exchange and consumption of information, which in turn becomes the prized commodity of new forms of capitalism that have been described variously as 'informational' (Castells 1996), fast (Agger 1991, 2004) and 'knowing' (Thrift 2005). Daniel Bell's writings on post-industrialism in the mid-1970s in many ways anticipated this idea of an information society, but it was from the mid-1990s onward, with the explosion of global information technologies such as the Internet, that this thesis became fully developed. But there is an irony here: while the term 'information society' has entered common parlance, the concept of information has received little detailed attention from within the discipline of sociology. This is especially the case in the writings of the key contemporary figure on this subject, Manuel Castells. For while Castells talks of 'information society' and 'informational society', there is barely a conceptual definition of the term 'information' to be found in his work. Castells deals with this question of definition in two footnotes in *The Information Age: Economy, Society and Culture*. In the first of these he says that

> [the] term 'information society' emphasizes the role of information in society. But I argue that information, in its broadest sense, e.g. as communication of knowledge, has been critical in all societies, including mediaeval Europe which was culturally structured, and to some extent unified, around scholasticism, that is, by and large an intellectual framework. In contrast, the term 'informational' indicates the attribute of a specific form of social organization in which information generation, processing, and transmission become the fundamental sources of productivity and power because of new technological conditions emerging in this historical period. (1996: 21)

What is interesting about this quote is his apparent dissatisfaction with the idea of 'information society'. In this passage, Castells sees information as something universal to all societies, thereby implying that 'information society' is in fact an empty term which fails to capture the 'productivity and power' of the digital age. In one respect, Castells is right: there is something qualitatively new about advanced capitalist societies in which accelerated capitalist and technological development both drive and feed back into each other, and in which the production and exchange of information assumes a new position of centrality. To see these developments as universal would indeed be a mistake. But Castells's frustration with the idea of 'information society' perhaps reveals something more: the difficulty of defining what exactly is meant by the term information in this context.

Castells struggles with precisely this task in a separate footnote, which is worth quoting in full:

> For the sake of clarity in this book, it is necessary to provide a definition of knowledge and information, even if such an intellectually satisfying gesture introduces a dose of the arbitrary in the discourse, as social scientists who have struggled with the issue know well. I have no compelling reason to improve on Daniel Bell's own definition of *knowledge*: 'Knowledge: a set of organized statements of facts or ideas, presenting a reasoned judgement or an experimental result, which is transmitted to others through some communication medium in some systematic form. Thus I distinguish knowledge from entertainment.' As for *information*, some established authors in the field, such as Machlup, simply define information as the communication of knowledge. However, this

is because Machlup's definition of knowledge seems excessively broad, as Bell argues. Thus, I would rejoin the operational definition of information proposed by Porat in his classic work: 'Information is data that have been organized and communicated.' (1996: 17)

There are two key arguments forwarded in the above passage. The first is that there exists a basic distinction between knowledge on one hand, and information on the other. This distinction lies at the centre of much of the literature in this field (see below), but is far from clear in Castells's account. It is difficult to discern, for example, what exactly distinguishes knowledge as 'a set of organized statements of facts or ideas' from information as 'data that have been organized and communicated'. It is equally unclear why this latter definition from Porat is indeed an advance over Machlup's 'excessively broad' idea that information is 'the communication of knowledge'. The second argument, which again comes from Daniel Bell, is that knowledge is 'transmitted to others through some communication medium in some systematic form'. This suggests that knowledge is somehow tied to *communication*. But again, this poses more questions than Castells answers. For example, why exactly does knowledge only become such when 'transmitted to others through some communication medium'? And how, as McLuhan asks, do media shape the packaging, transmission and consumption of knowledge? For if knowledge cannot exist outside media, do dramatic changes in media technologies bring accompanying transformations in the form of knowledge itself? These questions are not addressed in any detail by Castells, but they are important nonetheless. In addition, it is worth noting that Castells's sources for defining knowledge and information all date from the pre-Internet era, namely Daniel Bell's *The Coming of Post-Industrial Society* (1976), Fritz Machlup's *The Production and Distribution of Knowledge in the United States* (1962) and Marc Porat's *The Information Economy* (1977). If, as McLuhan and even Bell suggests, knowledge is framed by the technologies through which it is produced and communicated, then perhaps a new definition of knowledge and information is needed in the light of recent technological developments. For surely knowledge and information (and the connection between the two) have altered in form and content with the onset of the digital age?

This is precisely the question that forms the focal point of Jean-François Lyotard's *Postmodern Condition*, which, although written back in 1979, opens with the stark observation that knowledge 'cannot survive unchanged' in a world of computerized capitalism. Lyotard, like Castells, takes Daniel Bell's writings on post-industrial society as a starting point, but his key point of interest is exactly how knowledge and information change with the advent of new communications technologies, and how these changes are tied to the dynamics of the capitalist market. In similar fashion to Castells, Lyotard observes that knowledge is becoming an 'informational commodity' (an argument still powerful today if we consider everyday examples such as store credit or loyalty cards that gather information about our purchases). But, unlike Castells, Lyotard pushes this idea further to suggest that the status of knowledge in the digital age is changing, for increasingly it is a compressed form that is designed to fit the media channels of the new capitalist marketplace. This is made possible by the reduction of knowledge to information or 'bits' so that they can be processed by machines, which in turn enable the high-speed transmission, exchange and consumption of data. In the light of this, Lyotard defines information as knowledge that is designed to 'fit into the new channels, and become operational' (1984: 4). Tiziana Terranova explains: 'For Lyotard, information refers to a mode of knowledge that is no longer reflective or contemplative but performative and pragmatic' (2006: 287). Lyotard's definition of information is thus quite close to that suggested by McLuhan, for it is a form of code or data that is non-discursive in form and which is produced (like short TV soundbytes) to be consumed by humans as if they were machines. Lyotard finds this reduction of knowledge to bits – 'the unit of information' – deeply disturbing. In *The Inhuman*, he reflects that

> [w]hen we're dealing with bits, there's no longer any question of free forms given here and now to sensibility and imagination. On the contrary, they are units of information conceived by computer engineering and definable at all linguistic levels – lexical, syntactic, rhetorical and the rest. They are assembled into systems following a set of possibilities (a 'menu') under the control of a programmer. (Lyotard 1993: 34)

Case Study: Facebook

Social networking sites are moving rapidly into the cultural mainstream. As of January 2008, one of the leading sites – Facebook – has more than 64 million users, and since January 2007 has had an average of 250,000 new registrations per day. It has 65 billion page views per month, and more than 14 million photos are uploaded to its site daily. The scale and pace of this development is astounding. At the heart of Facebook, however is something that is seemingly mundane: the personal profile. This profile is assembled by the user and contains details of the network to which we belong (the primary category), followed by our sex, relationship status, political views and religious and consumer preferences. While mundane, these are important informational sources that enable connections to be made between people with similar tastes and preferences, and, at a deeper level, are of significant economic value. In late 2007, *The Financial Times* reported Facebook to be worth around US$15 billion. One driver for this valuation is advertising (which is rumoured to net in excess of US$1.5 million a week), but it is the user-generated information that is held

The key point of this passage is that information is different from traditional forms of knowledge that demand human creativity and reflection, for it has become the currency of a computer-based capitalism that prioritizes the speed and efficiency of data transmission over all else. In sum, for Lyotard, information is knowledge produced for the accelerated capitalist marketplace: it is cheap to produce, easy to exchange, and fast to consume and throw away.

This distinction between knowledge as a discursive, narrative-based form and information as a collection of fast-moving bits plays out in a slightly different way in the work of Scott Lash. Lash, in his work *Critique of Information*, does not draw directly on the work of Lyotard, but makes a comparable distinction between narrative-based knowledge which demands patient meditation and reflection, and faster, technologized forms of information that disappear often as quickly as they emerge. Lash states that

> [p]reviously the dominant medium was narrative, lyric poetry, discourse, the painting. But now it is the message: the message or the 'communication'. The medium is very byte-like. It is compressed. The newspaper already gave the model for the information age. Only now it has become much more pervasive and has spread to a whole series of mostly machinic interfaces. (2002: 2)

Lash, like Lyotard and also McLuhan, says little about the actual content of information (if indeed it has a content in any traditional sense), but focuses instead on the form it has to take in order for it to flow through and be produced by digital communications media. Whereas traditional paper-based forms of knowledge tend to

---

by Facebook that is perhaps its greatest financial asset. In 2007, Facebook began to generate revenues by developing advertising informed by user activities and preferences. This caused significant disquiet among the users of these free-to-access spaces (see the controversy over Facebook Beacon at http://en.wikipedia.org/wiki/ Facebook_Beacon), but is one instance of a much wider movement toward what Lyotard and others see as the commodification of information. This process might be explored in a contemporary setting by asking a number of key questions of social networking sites such as Facebook. For example, why is the information stored on such sites so economically valuable? How might such information be used, or how is it already being used, by commercial organizations to generate revenue? Should we be concerned about giving up personal data freely, and exactly who owns such data? Finally, at a grander level, are 'free' social networking sites user-owned, or are they spaces through which the forces of big capital are further extending into our everyday lives?

be slow to produce, transmit and consume, what distinguishes contemporary forms of information is their ease and speed of movement. Lash observes, for example, that information is marked by the 'primary qualities' of 'flow, disembeddedness, spatial compression, temporal compression, real-time relations' (2002). Lash depicts information as presentational rather than representational, arguing that it contains messages in their 'brute facticity'. An example might be a live stream of share price data that is fed directly from the market. Such data – in this case a fast-moving array of numbers on a screen – has no clear narrative or discursive form but has to be understood in its immediacy as it emerges and changes at an accelerated rate across time. The challenge of reading such data is to make sense of bytes of information that are constantly changing and which on their own might mean nothing at all.

The challenge, then, is of how information is to be *decoded*. Shunya Yoshimi, a key figure in Japanese information studies, sees this as returning us to the question of form: 'Information is the process of "giving form to something". It involves finding patterns or reading messages in the objects of observation (whether these be natural or social phenomena)' (2006: 271). The physicist Hans von Baeyer takes a similar position, that

> [i]nformation is the . . . infusion of form on some previously unformed entity, just as de-, con-, trans-, and re-formation refer to the undoing, copying, changing, and renewing of forms. Information refers to moulding or shaping a formless heap – imposing a form onto something. (2003: 20)

He adds that: 'Information is the transfer of form from one medium to another' (2003: 25). Information, then, is always *in-formation*: it is about the movement of data or codes through a range of different communications media, and about the struggle to find a form or narrative to make such movement intelligible.

Lash points out, however, that there is little time for such reflection in a techno-capitalist world in which the production and exchange of information plays out at an accelerated rate. This in turn presents a further difficulty for social and cultural theorists: how is critique of the information order to take place when there is little time or space for creative action: for reading, writing and, above all, critical reflection. This loss of critical distance or space is Lash's main concern, for he sees no outside to this order, and hence no transcendental or separate space from which critique, in the traditional sense, may be launched. Lash's response to this situation is to assert that critique is to come from *within* the dominant information system. For this to happen, however, a rethinking not just of theory but also of what is meant by culture and 'the social' is needed. For Lash, no longer is culture a representational form that is easy to separate from the social and economic spheres (if indeed it ever was). Rather, both culture and the social have become technologized: the 'cultural superstructure' has become 'part and parcel of the economic base' (Lash 2002: 76), while at the same time new media technologies are now to be found 'at the heart of the social'. This means, in turn, that traditional forms of understanding and critique have lost both their ground and their object of study, for there is now seen to be nothing outside of technology.

In the face of this difficulty, Lash takes on the task of reformulating critical theory in the information age. He suggests that social theory should learn from new media theory, which not only places new media at the centre of study (thereby treating sociality and culture largely as after-effects), but also follows these media in becoming a technological form or device in itself. Such theory, he writes,

> neither explains nor interprets the media. It explodes the binary opposition between explanation and interpretation ... In the new set of arrangements, media are no longer 'texts' or narratives or pictorial representations ... Theories and texts now become ... technologies themselves. Text and theory become objects in today's generalized global networks of flow and dispersion of the whole variety of objects. Only these texts, these theories are a bit longer lasting than the other circulating objects. (Lash 2002: 76–7)

Media theory thus takes critical theory in a new direction, into what Lash calls *informationcritique*. As implied by the fusion of these terms, such a practice involves a critique of information in which there is no separation between the critique and its object. Such critique, he argues, is not merely fast but informational: it comes from within the information order while at the same time seeking to turn the logic of this order against itself.

CONCLUSION

Perhaps the most obvious conclusion to be drawn from this chapter is that the concept of information eludes simple definition. Information is a perfect illustration of Deleuze and Guattari's argument (discussed in **Chapter 1**) that concepts are not simple entities but rather multiplicities that can take on many different meanings. There is no single concept of information, but rather many that have emanated from a range of different disciplinary sources, including computer science, media studies and sociology. Our argument, beyond this, is that no existing definition of information is, on its own, sufficient. The conceptual definition of information forwarded by cybernetic theorists such as Shannon and Weaver, for example, says little about how information is part of the everyday dynamics of contemporary capitalist society and culture (as addressed by thinkers such as Lyotard). This same criticism might be levelled at media theorists such as McLuhan, Kittler and Hayles.

By contrast, theories of 'information society' forwarded by thinkers such as Castells tend to lack a clear definition of what information is, and the technical procedures through which it is produced, materialized and embodied. This rather confusing picture leaves us with a number of partial accounts that it is tempting to work into a conceptual whole. But such synthesis is not likely to be an easy task, for the definition of these concepts by thinkers as far removed as Shannon, Kittler, Haraway or Castells takes place in very different epistemological and political frameworks that are in many ways mutually exclusive. For example, Shannon and Kittler emphasize the primacy of the information system over questions of human agency, while Hayles seeks to reveal the liberal presuppositions that underpin the cybernetic definition of information in terms of choice, and Castells (2001) seeks to reassert agency of the human actor within what he calls the 'Internet galaxy'. Against this backdrop, perhaps the best that can be hoped for is a reworking of this concept that remains sensitive to the engineering, embodiment *and* commodification of information. This is beyond the scope of the present chapter, but by way of conclusion it might be observed that there are other important considerations that could inform such a rethinking. Lash's idea of information critique and Haraway's theory of techno-biopower, for example, could be fused with recent empirically informed sociological analyses of the digital divide (see Loader and Keeble 2004; Crang et al. 2006). Questions might then be asked about the role information plays in dividing or sorting populations, and about the potential connections between information processing technologies and new possibilities for the classification, surveillance and ultimately governance of different social groups (Burrows and Gane, 2006). Such questions might, in turn, form the basis of a critical theory of both information and information society.

Chapter Summary

- Little critical attention has been paid to the concept of information that underpins contemporary arguments about 'information society'.
- In early information science and cybernetic theory information is defined in mathematical or statistical terms (Shannon and Weaver).
- Against this, there has been a move to assert the materiality or embodiment of information (Kittler, Hayles).
- Information is *the* key commodity of advanced capitalism (Lyotard).
- Critical theory, and more fundamentally the idea of critique, is to be reconfigured if it is to be effective in the information age (Lash).

4 INTERFACE

> Provisionally we may say that the interface stands between the human and the machinic, a kind of membrane dividing yet connecting two worlds that are alien to and also dependent upon each other.
>
> Poster (1996: 20)

In recent years, the concept of the interface has taken on increasing analytic significance as commentators have attempted to understand connections between the human and the machine, and the so-called virtual and the physical. Interfaces are important conceptual devices that enable us to think across and beyond such dualisms by calling attention to the common boundaries 'between two systems, devices, or programs' (Illingworth and Pyle 2004), and to the forms of contact that might be possible if such boundaries are negotiated and/or transgressed. Mark Poster expresses this as follows: 'interfaces of high quality allow seamless crossings between ... two worlds, thereby facilitating the disappearance of the difference between them and thereby, as well, altering the type of linkage between the two' (Poster 1996: 21). The interface is the point at which information is 'instantiated', to use Hayles's (1999) terminology, or where the organic and inorganic come together to form the cybernetic, if we return to the writings of Haraway. The argument of the present chapter is that understanding the role that the interface plays in such processes is crucial, especially if we wish to concern ourselves, as Haraway has recommended, with the politics of information or *informatics* that reside at commonplace points of contact between humans and machines.

This focus on interfaces, on points of contact at which different bodily or machinic systems meet, shifts the agenda of new media theory away from simply the analysis of network structures (analysed in detail in **Chapter 2**) toward the understanding of how these take form and are made possible. Interfaces are conceptual and material devices that occupy and enable key points of contact within networks, and because of this might be studied to gain an understanding of how new media operate and the effects that they produce (Beer 2008). For if we wish to see how connections between different systems are forged and are subsequently incorporated into networks

(**Chapter 2**), how information and various bodily and technical materialities are interwoven (**Chapter 3**), or how new media devices provide 'interactive' experiences (**Chapter 6**), then analysing the concept of interface might prove to be a fruitful exercise. Perhaps the most important quality of interfaces is that they navigate boundaries between different objects and systems, and in the process not only enable networks to operate but also to extend into new terrain, and thereby grow. It is thus not far-fetched to claim that interfaces are to be found at the very centre of new media systems and infrastructures. Even a cursory glance around public and private spaces reveals the range of interfaces that are today woven into our everyday lives, including the interfaces of mobile phones, laptops, personal digital assistants, MP3 players and so on. Given this centrality it is surprising how little detailed attention the interface has received to date. To guide our analysis in this chapter, we take the following question as our point of departure: what is an interface and how can it be used as a concept for understanding our points of contact with informational or networked systems? We will seek to answer this question by addressing three main bodies of literature on new media interfaces. The first concerns their operation as cultural devices, the second their connection to mobile forms of power and surveillance, and the third the ways in which they mediate everyday experiences of social and physical space. From these three loosely defined approaches, questions of power and agency will emerge that we revisit throughout the rest of this book, and in particular in our analysis of interactivity (**Chapter 6**) and simulation (**Chapter 7**). Key points of concern, only some of which are touched upon in the present chapter, include the power of the interface to shape communication and information access, the networked connections – bodily, technical and spatial – that interfaces afford, and the agency of the user in his/her engagement with a range of different new media devices.

CULTURAL INTERFACES

To set the scene for the discussion that follows we begin with Steven Johnson's account of what he describes as 'interface culture'. Johnson says of the interface that

> In its simplest sense, the word refers to software that shapes the interaction between user and computer. The interface serves as a kind of translator, mediating between the two parties, making one sensible to the other. In other words, the relationship governed by the interface is a semantic one, characterized by meaning and expression rather than physical force. (1997: 14)

Defining the interface as an in-between or translational device provides a useful point of departure for this chapter. In these very broad terms, interfaces can be understood as places or surfaces where two bodies or systems come together: a human and a machine (our main focus here), two humans, or perhaps two machines. Interfaces enable the formation of networks across or between different beings, objects or media. Interfaces are thus not confined to new media, for we engage with people and technical objects frequently in our everyday lives, and not always through the use of digital technologies. Indeed, the term interface can be used to conceptualize engagements with all communications media – whether 'old' or 'new' (a distinction we will return to in the conclusion to this book: see **Chapter 8**). This is the position of Lev Manovich, who argues that traditional media such as books or magazines are interfaces through which users engage with written narratives or stories. He also gives the example of cinema: 'its physical interface is the particular architectural arrangement of the movie theatre' (Manovich 2001: 73). In this view, the foyer of the cinema, its information boards, the auditorium and the screen and speakers are all interfaces that shape our experience of film.

It is important, in view of the above, that we define our frame of reference, and be clear about the types of interface that we intend to study. This is particularly true if we begin to think of cinema, or maybe even a book or a pen, as types of interface. Our answer to this difficulty is that because this is a book about new media we will focus exclusively on interfaces that are points of contact between humans and digital technologies. But even if we narrow down our frame of reference in this way, there are still difficulties to be addressed. For example, which parts of computational machines, or even of the human body, constitute an interface? Computers are laden with so-called interfaces: the keyboard, mouse, touch-pad, screen, software, to name but a few. On the side of the human body we might ask whether the interface is the point at which, for example, the finger touches a computer mouse, or where the eye observes the images on the screen. (See for example the discussion in Hayles (1999) of 'flickering signifiers'.) One answer might be to think in terms of interfaces *within* interfaces: of sets of interfaces embedded within or working in conjunction with one another (in a similar sense to the concepts of this book). This approach is fitting, as new media systems are made up of many layers of interfaces that come into contact with one another, with outside networks and, in some cases, with human bodies. To simply things, it is perhaps best to begin with the notion that interfaces enable the flow of information between human bodies and different media machines. In so doing, they do not sit passively between such systems but to some extent become embodied within them. As we will see through the course of this and following chapters, different writers ascribe to the interface various levels of agency in this process. In some cases the interface is merely a membrane or a mediator, in others it is a site of constant and often concealed power, and in others again it plays a substantive role in shaping visions of so-called 'reality' (a point that is picked up in our analysis of simulation in **Chapter 7**).

A key text that helps address some of the above difficulties is Lev Manovich's *The Language of New Media* (2001), which analyses the conceptual underpinnings and the materialities of interfaces. In this work, Manovich develops an important observation: that the computer has become a filter for culture, and that practically all culture now passes through, or is capable of being passed through, a human-computer interface (the most popular being GUIs or Graphical User Interfaces). According to Manovich:

> The interface shapes how the computer user conceives of the computer itself. It also determines how users think of any media object accessed via a computer. Stripping different media of their original distinctions, the interface imposes its own logic on them. Finally, by organizing computer data in particular ways, the interface provides distinct models of the world. (2001: 65)

By extension, Manovich talks of 'cultural interfaces' or 'human-computer-culture interfaces' which structure 'the ways in which computers present and allow us to interact with cultural data' (2001: 70). For in using computers we are not simply interfacing with a machine but interfacing more broadly with culture, even if this culture is encoded in digital form. The following instances are cited by Manovich as examples: 'the interfaces used by the designers of Web sites, CD-ROM and DVD titles, multimedia encyclopaedias, on-line museums and magazines, computer games, and other new media cultural objects' (Manovich 2001). Each of these inter-faces presents itself as something new insofar as it mediates human access to culture through a digital technology: the computer. For Manovich, this process of inter-facing, while appearing to break from previous media traditions, is nothing exactly new, as human-computer interfaces are themselves the product of previous cultural forms or interfaces, most notably the written word, cinema and the 'general-purpose human-computer interface (HCI) or, a general-purpose tool which can be used to manipulate any kind of data' (2001: 72).

So-called 'new' media are often developments or remediations of previous tech-nological forms. (For more on remediation and the separation of old and new media see **Chapters 6** and **8**, and Bolter and Grusin (1999).) Of these, cinema is, for Manovich, the most significant, for with the emergence of new GUIs he argues that audio-visual representation has taken over from text as the dominant cultural interface or 'language' of media. He writes: 'A hundred years after cinema's birth, cinematic ways of seeing the world, of structuring time, of narrating a story, of link-ing one experience to the next, have become the basic means by which computer users access and interact with all cultural data' (Manovich 2001: 79). More strongly, he adds that

> [element] by element, cinema is being poured into a computer: first, one-point linear perspective; next, the mobile camera and rectangular window; next, cinematography and editing conventions; and, of course, digital personas based on acting conventions borrowed from cinema to be followed by make-up, set design, and the narrative structures themselves. Rather than being merely one cultural language among others, cinema is now becoming *the* cultural interface, a toolbox for all cultural communication, overtaking the printed word. (2001: 86)

Cinema thus gains a new lease of life: it becomes 'the toolbox of the computer user' and is reborn as a new kind of cultural interface (pp. 287–333).

A key aspect of this process is that it involves a degree of standardization, particularly as interfaces used en masse tend to contain many of the same features or controls. Manovich, however, sees no overriding tendency toward cultural homogenization in this process, even though he detects the emergence of a new 'cultural metalanguage' (2001: 93). For although new media interfaces are 'widely used and easily learned' (p. 79), their language, in spite of its cinematic leaning and remediated history, remains a hybrid form: 'a strange, often awkward mix between the conventions of traditional cultural forms and the conventions of HCI – between an immersive environment and a set of controls, between standardization and originality' (Manovich 2001: 91). Instead of casting a final judgement on the outcome of this play between control and openness, Manovich suggests that this environment, as a 'new' form, has yet to stabilize, with the consequence that it is hard, if not impossible, to judge the outcome of its development. But one thing seems certain for Manovich: the continuing influence of cinema on the emerging form of cultural interfaces. For in spite of the development of virtual reality (VR) and simulation technologies, new media interfaces remain tied to the medium of the screen (2001: 115), even if this medium is itself changing in form – becoming larger and more difficult to move in the case of computer and TV screens, and smaller and more mobile in the case of VR machines, palmtops and mobile phones.

Issues of originality and control return in Manovich's analysis of the application or 'operation' layer of new media. This analysis focuses not on the workings of specific applications, such as Microsoft Word or Adobe Photoshop, but on three 'general techniques' or commands that are common in such applications: selection, compositing and teleaction. Each of these techniques is taken to be of cultural interest insofar as it is more than simply a technical operation: all of them are, rather, 'general ways of working, of thinking, and ways of existing in a computer age' (Manovich

2001: 118). They are said to be 'new' insofar as they obey the most general, technical principle of new media: 'transcoding'. Manovich explains: 'operations should be seen as another case of … transcoding. Encoding in algorithms and implemented as software commands, operations exist independently of the media data to which they can be applied' (2001: 121). In the case of the first, and most interesting, of the above techniques, *selection*, Manovich declares that a further principle is central: variability. This is because new media are designed less to enable us to create cultural objects from scratch than to assemble them from ready-made parts. This process is again nothing essentially new, but, as Manovich explains, it is made simple with the advent of the networked computer:

> The practice of putting together a media object from already existing commer-cially distributed media elements existed with old media, but new media technology made it much easier to perform. What before involved scissors and glue now involves clicking on 'cut' and 'paste'. And, by encoding the operations of selection and combination into the very interfaces of authoring and editing software, new media 'legitimizes' them. Pulling elements from databases and libraries becomes the default; creating them from scratch becomes the exception. The Web acts as a perfect materialization of this logic. It is one gigantic library of graphics, photographs, video, audio, design layouts, software code, and texts; and every element is free because it can be saved to the user's computer with a single mouse click. (2001: 130)

This idea of 'every element' being 'free' is not exactly true, for of course some images, texts, codes must be paid for in order to be downloaded. For Manovich, however, this is not the key point. Rather, it is how authorship – and with this creativity and originality – has changed with the emergence of new media (something we return to in our analysis of the archive in **Chapter 5**).

The key development is that ready-made, partially assembled or composited forms take precedence over creation from scratch. This development would appear to be a liberating force as anyone with a computer can, with little skill, achieve effects that were previously restricted to the realm of the expert (for example, the use of filters to manipulate an image in Adobe Photoshop). To an extent, Manovich agrees that this is the case, arguing that the operations of new media technologies close the gap between work and leisure, authors and readers, producers and users, and, to an extent, professionals and amateurs (2001: 119). At the same time, however, he is reluctant to endorse new media technologies as emancipatory forces. For, in line with his position on interactivity (see **Chapter 6**), he sees a certain set of social norms built into the design of application-based operations. He never details exactly what these norms are, where they come from or why they prevail, but instead takes 'the logic of selection' as a 'good example':

a set of social and economic practices and conventions is now encoded in the software design itself. The result is a new form of control, soft but powerful. Although software does not directly prevent its users from creating from scratch, its design on every level makes it 'natural' to follow a different logic – that of selection. (Manovich 2001: 129)

This implies that a control structure is built into the fabric of new technology media – a structure that naturalizes automated ways of thinking and working, while at the same time reducing interactivity to the adoption of 'already pre-established identities' (Manovich 2001). This is something to which we will return in detail in **Chapters 6** and 7.

In a final twist, however, Manovich drifts away from analysis of this connection between power and new media technology to look instead at the images and illusions created by the use of digital media. In the process he all but reverses his previous position by arguing that new media technologies in fact transform visual images into truly interactive forms: '*new media turn most images into image-interfaces and image-instruments*' (2001: 183, emphasis in original). He explains that

[the] image becomes interactive, that is, it now functions as an interface between a user and a computer or other devices. The user employs an *image-interface* to control a computer, asking it to zoom into the image or display another one, start a software application, connect to the Internet, and so on. The user employs *image-instruments* to directly affect reality – move a robotic arm in a remote location, fire a missile, change the speed of a car and set the temperature, and so on. To evoke a term often used in film theory, new media moves us from identification to action. (2001)

Suddenly, all talk of manipulation or control is dropped. For rather than focusing on the limitations of menu-based interactivity or automated forms of selection, Manovich argues that new media images become interfaces and, particularly in the form of computer games or virtual reality, become sites of high (inter-)activity. Humans are said to 'control' the computer through the use of the interface, rather than vice versa, and as a consequence viewers become 'active users'. In other words, not only do the actual images that constitute interfaces become highly interactive forms, but the interfaces themselves become *instruments* that allow us to construct and manipulate the appearance of what might be called 'reality' (a question that lies at the centre of our analysis of simulation in **Chapter** 7).

This change of tack is frustrating, as it appears inconsistent with the position we outlined at the outset of this section. Equally frustrating is Manovich's attempt to analyse new media devices in their own technical terms, and through a technical history of remediation rather than in relation to wider processes of social or cultural change, in particular to the changing dynamics of contemporary capitalism. But there are strengths to Manovich's account, the main one being that it is not simply dazzled by recent technological innovations. He instead looks to persuade the reader of the breaks *and* continuities between different media technologies. Manovich reminds us, for example, that 'the language of cultural interfaces is largely made up from elements of other, already familiar cultural forms' (Manovich 2001: 71). Manovich is a vocal proponent of this position, which insists that new media are to be understood in relation to their historical emergence and development.

Manovich is not alone in taking this line. As well as work by Silverstone and Graham that we will address in **Chapters 6** and **8**, Katherine Hayles also argues that illustrations of a technical history can often be found residing in the interface. In particular, she calls attention to the 'skeumorph': a 'design feature that is no longer functional in itself but that refers back to a feature that was functional at an earlier time' (Hayles 1999: 17). Hayles illustrates this point through the example of imitation stitching that one might find on a car dashboard. Such stitching was once a part of the material construction of the car, but is now an aesthetic form – a symbolic gesture back to a previous and now outdated functionality. It is in such skeumorphs that we can see a history of the evolution of technical objects in which the previous technical forms hang over into the present, and in the process take on new materialities and meanings. Viewed in this way, interfaces can contain non-functional aspects that are part of their remediated histories. Understanding this process of remediation – both material and symbolic or aesthetic – has become a dominant theme in attempts to analyse interfaces from a cultural perspective, or

---

Case Study: The iPod and the iPhone

The iPod, launched by Apple in November 2001, has become an 'icon' of the digital age, and today continues to be one of the most widely used technologies for storing and retrieving music, photos and videos while on the move. On 9 April 2007, Apple announced that it had sold its 100 millionth iPod player, and that the associated iTunes portal had sold an estimated 2.5 billion songs. In late 2007, Apple launched its iPhone, which incorporates mobile phone technology and wireless web access with an iPod music player. This development is an example of media convergence — where the form of previous media becomes embedded as content of new media, and where different media devices extend their functionality through the use of a common user-interface. One of the new features of the iPhone is that the user-interface it employs is near-invisible: the touch screen. This interface is easy to take for granted because it is physically transparent and creates the feeling of a near-seamless interplay between the body and the machine (with the user's finger sliding across the screen to operate virtual controls). Such interfaces also tend to conceal the uses of, and practices associated with,

more broadly to think of 'interface culture' (Johnson 1997) as a form of remediated culture. As new media interfaces have become woven into the bodily and/or spatial materialities of everyday life, they have also been described as being 'ubiquitous' or 'pervasive'. It is to this aspect of new media interfaces that we now turn.

PERVASIVE INTERFACES

While Manovich focuses primarily on the technical design and operation of different media interfaces, a literature is currently emerging that presents the interface as spatial form that is tied to a broader set of social and cultural dynamics. A key argument is that mobile interfaces are becoming increasingly ubiquitous across and within the spaces of everyday life (Anne Galloway 2004; Beer 2007). This development is, to some extent, anticipated by Donna Haraway in her *Cyborg Manifesto* (originally published in 1985), in which she argues that the 'home, workplace, market, public arena, the body itself – all can be dispersed and interfaced in nearly infinite, polymorphous ways' (Haraway 1991: 163). She continues, 'no objects, spaces, or bodies are sacred in themselves; any component can be interfaced with any other if the proper standard, the proper code, can be constructed for processing signals in a common language' (Haraway 1991). This prediction of the seamless connection between different media has not quite been realized (even if it is there in potential), for it has been tempered by a push by the capitalist marketplace to take proprietary control of its networks and the devices they connect. This has been achieved with varying degrees of success through the hard-wiring of certain media so that they

the device itself. For example, interfaces between the iPod, bodies and other machines underpin the following practices but are rarely considered in their own right: ripping music from CDs, buying songs online, file-sharing, the docking of the iPod with one of the many speaker systems on the market, and the 'syncing' of devices through the use of a home computer. These practices are made possible by a range of technical interfaces that are governed by protocols (see *Chapter 2*), and each raises interesting questions about the meeting points of, and connections between, information, the body and the physical environments in which they are situated. As media devices become increasingly convergent and integrated into everyday bodily practices these questions become more complex. One way of approaching a simple and sleek interface like the iPod or iPhone is perhaps to see it as portal into a complex set of social relations, technical infrastructures and cultural practices that we might want to unpick to create a richer understanding of the role that interfaces, and new media technologies more generally, play in our everyday lives.

are only interfaceable through adherence to specific platforms and protocols. An example of this is the locking of mobile phones (such as the iPhone) so that they can only be used with SIM cards supplied by particular network providers. This, in turn, has given rise to a new culture and business of hacking and 'unlocking'. But in other respects, Haraway has been proved right, for we have also witnessed the emergence of new open networks and archives (see **Chapter 5**) which are not simply dominated by the interests of big capital, and which can be interfaced through any device that is web-enabled. Moreover, even where the commercial interests are present, there is often a striking degree of compatibility between rival networks, systems and platforms that enables media devices to communicate with each other.

One consequence is that new media interfaces are becoming increasingly pervasive or ubiquitous in everyday life. This is not to say that mobile communication devices abstract life from its immediate surroundings – the so-called end of geography thesis – but rather that they mesh bodies with concrete spaces in new ways (Mitchell 2003), and give rise to new forms of spatial information, or what Mitchell (2005) calls 'urban information overlays'. Such meshing has become possible largely because of the miniaturization of the physical form of new media to the extent that we now hardly notice them. This, again, has been anticipated by Haraway: 'microelectronic devices are everywhere and they are invisible' (Haraway 1991: 153). New media and their interfaces are becoming ever more compact, and with this 'eminently portable' (Haraway 1991). The point has even arrived at which we may wear or even implant these technologies. Nigel Thrift, for example talks of 'nascent local intelligence' and of the possibility of creating 'computationally active textiles which are able to weave the circuit into cloth' (2005: 162). He adds that 'though commercial wearables will at first consist of … little more than bulky multipocketed jackets able to contain various pieces of electronic kit, the future might be very different' (Thrift 2005).

Such developments sit alongside the emergence of a range of other 'intelligent' technologies or 'things that think' (Mitchell 2005: 61), in particular the radio frequency identification (RFID) tag (see Beer 2007): a 'pinhead-sized wireless transponder that costs pennies and can be embedded in just about anything, from consumer products to pets' (Mitchell 2005: 61). These devices are so small and cheap to produce that they have the potential to go anywhere and be 'invisibly embedded into virtually any object' (Anne Galloway 2004: 389; see Thrift 2005: 222). These technologies work as follows: 'you ping a RFID tag with a suitable RF (radio frequency) signal, it returns a unique ID number. Thus it is much like the familiar barcode, except that it can be read silently, invisibly, and at a distance' (Mitchell 2005: 62). The implication is that things, spaces and even bodies become networked, often without the knowledge or awareness of the users involved. This in turn gives rise to unprecedented capacities for surveillance and control, for RFID technologies now allow physical objects and bodies to be positioned and tracked through the Internet, and for real-time 'information about them to be both collected and delivered' (Mitchell 2005: 63). This development has been characterized in terms of the emergence of an 'Internet of things' (see for example http://www.internet-of-things-2008.org/), and is currently arousing critical attention from within the social and cultural sciences (see for example Gane, Venn and Hand 2007; Crang and Graham 2007). Mitchell's prediction is that soon near-invisible RFID tags will be 'everywhere'. As evidence for this he observes that Gillette recently ordered 'half a billion of them to embed in razorblade packages and other such products' (Mitchell 2005: 63). These devices are part of a broader shift to a world of 'intelligent environments' (Thrift 2005) in which things 'think a little more' (Mitchell 2005: 63). Mitchell observes, for example, that in the case of RFID tags 'you can provide them with onboard processing power, wireless communication capability, and the capacity to self-organize themselves into wireless sensor nets' (2005). This extends the computational power and informational outputs of RFID technology, enabling it to mesh with a greater range of applications while also enhancing the ability of these networked devices to organize or think around connections. This connectivity of things, spaces and bodies has daunting consequences, not least because, as Mitchell observes, it can 'continuously track your behaviour, draw inferences from it, and anticipate your needs' (2003: 60).

The power of such devices and their near-invisible interfaces is enhanced, in turn, by the emergence of new technologies for data storage and mining: technologies that can amass and sift huge quantities of data in order to identify trends that may otherwise be invisible to the human eye. Mitchell conceives of a potential intersection between data mining applications and RFID tags through a commonly used image of a thinking building. He explains that

> RFID tags, sensors, distributed intelligence, and wireless networking technologies are combining to create the possibility of buildings that continually draw inferences about their inhabitants and respond accordingly. In Cambridge, Massachusetts ... architect Kent Larson is currently constructing PlaceLab – an apartment that thinks – to critically explore the implications of this. PlaceLab is loaded with tags and sensors, and harvests an enormous flood of information, which is then mined for inferences about the current condition and needs of its inhabitants. (2005: 63)

Such networks of 'intelligent' devices and interfaces might be put to work in a variety of different ways. For example, we can imagine fridges and cupboards that order food as stocks get low (Mitchell 2003: 119), heating and lighting systems that respond to patterns of behaviour and the changing conditions of the external environment, or home gymnasium equipment that relays information about our fitness to doctors or personal trainers. These examples may appear banal, but nonetheless they raise important questions about the changing nature of power and privacy, especially if we consider where information generated by these devices is stored, who has access to it, and to what wider (commercial) purposes it can be applied. Katherine Hayles (2007: 349) is one among many to have voiced concerns here: 'As RFID moves into the environment and becomes pervasive, it will in my view pose unprecedented challenges and opportunities to humans because they will be moving within an intelligent and context-aware environment'. For with the emergence of technologies such as RFID, *the interface becomes increasingly ambient and unseen*, leaving us unaware that our bodies and possessions might be feeding data about our movements and habits to back-end databases. This has led many to question the political and ethical consequences of RFID and related technologies, most notably organisations such as CASPIAN (Consumers Against Supermarket Privacy Invasion and Numbering) (see http://www.nocards.org/). At stake here is the politics of an interface that is so seamlessly embedded within the objects of everyday life that it conceals its own presence, together with its underlying purpose and workings.

URBAN INFORMATICS

A key aspect of the pervasiveness of interfaces is their near-seamless positioning within everyday spaces and places, something that has recently become of interest to those working in the field known as urban informatics. This again returns us to the urban media theory of Mitchell, which picks up on motifs in Haraway's work and uses them to consider the ways in which new media devices mesh together bodies, objects and places to produce new configurations of time and space. At the outset of Mitchell's book *ME++*, he reflects that this has much to do with underlying processes of miniaturization:

> In my hand I held an inexpensive transmitter and receiver that was immeasurably more sophisticated than Marconi's immense construction, and could instantly connect me to any one of hundreds of millions of similar devices scattered around the world. Furthermore, it could link me to the countless servers of the Internet and the Web, I pulled off the cover (no doubt voiding the warranty) to reveal a palm-sized, precisely made architectural model; the powerhouse had shrunk to a matchbook-scaled battery, the transmission house now resided on a chip, and the antenna tower was just a couple of inches long ... the device that I now grasped was a liberating extension of my mobile body. (2003: 2)

In this passage, Mitchell describes the interface as a kind of prosthesis that is integrated into the physical and informational (infra)structures of city space. This marks the emergence of an extended and networked cyborg body that is defined by ubiquity, miniaturization and above all mobility. Mitchell explains that

> the body/city metaphors have turned concrete and literal. Embedded within a vast structure of nested boundaries and ramifying networks, my muscular and skeletal, physiological, and nervous systems have been artificially augmented and expanded. My reach extends indefinitely and interacts with the similarly extended reaches of others to produce a global system of transfer, actuation, sensing, and control. My biological body mashes with the city; the city itself has become not only the domain of my networked cognitive system, but also – and crucially – the spatial and material embodiment of that system. (2003: 19)

The body, in this account, becomes woven into the informational and material structures of the city as mobile networked devices blur traditional boundary lines between ourselves and our lived environments by placing us in 'a state of continuous electronic engagement' with our surroundings (Mitchell 2003: 2).

On this basis, it is possible to argue that the new media interface is the meeting point of a number of important social and cultural dynamics, for it enables and mediates informational power structures, restructures everyday practices in a myriad of ways, and transforms relations between bodies and their environments. Perhaps the best way forward is to avoid thinking of interfaces in isolation as discrete technologies in their own right, and to conceive of them instead as membranes or mediating devices that are not only integrated into our everyday routines, but tied to a deeper set of social and cultural processes. While media interfaces are commonly depicted as iconic symbols of the digital age, behind this image is a complex intersection of social practices and technical infrastructures (see Beer 2008). As interfaces embed themselves in the everyday, increasingly they 'define our perceptions of the space we inhabit, as well as the type of interaction with other people with whom we might connect' (de Souza e Silva 2006: 261). Pervasive and locational interfaces do a number of things: they help organize social connections, they retrieve information and feed it to our senses, and forge new relations with our lived environments. (We can see links here with Baudrillard's vision of simulation as discussed in **Chapter 7**.)

These processes are central concerns of urban informatics, and are also addressed by contemporary work on ubiquitous computing, which tends to take the interface, and particularly its design, as the focal point of analysis (Anne Galloway 2004; Kirkpatrick 2004; de Souza e Silva 2006). Adriana de Souza e Silva defines interfaces as 'communication mediators, representing information between two parts, making them meaningful to one another' (2006: 261). What is interesting about this definition is that it is framed not by Manovich's idea of 'cultural interfaces', which is concerned primarily with the technical structures that underpin the interface and its use, but by a theory of the 'social interface' which asks how the interface is connected to its place of operation and how it frames everyday sociality. The starting point of de Souza e Silva's position is that the 'the role of the interface is to translate digital information from computers to humans to make it understandable to us' (2006). The interface is a translational device that operates between machines or between humans and machines to produce information that is mutually compatible. de Souza e Silva goes a step further to propose a

> conceptualization of the 'social interface', which defines a digital device that
> intermediates relationships between two or more users. Within this context,
> social interfaces not only reshape communication relationships but also reshape
> the space in which this interaction takes place. (2006: 262)

We can begin to see how the interface plays a crucial part in enabling the formation of social networks, not least because it mediates between individuals and wider groups of users. This is something that we will consider in further detail in our analysis of Web 2.0 in the following chapter. De Souza e Silva, meanwhile, refers to the mobile phone as a key example: 'Formerly regarded as mobile telephones, these devices can now be increasingly compared to microcomputers, remote controls, and collective social devices' (2006). What is at stake here is not just new media and their interfaces mediating social relationships and networks, but also something deeper: the problematization of what might be considered as 'social' in such a landscape (see Gane 2004: 1–16). For as de Souza e Silva rightly observes, 'every shift in the meaning of an interface requires a reconceptualisation of the type of social relationships and spaces it mediates' (2006: 262).

This complex interplay between the social and the technological is not something we can explore in any detail in the course of the present chapter. Rather, what might be observed is the importance of social and physical space in the agenda of ubiquitous computing in general, and in de Souza e Silva's work in particular. A key argument is that the mobile and networked interface, by feeding information into lived environments, creates new 'hybrid spaces' that integrate virtual and physical spaces, thereby rendering the two almost inseparable. It is possible, in turn, that this image of 'hybrid space' may provide a useful alternative to visions of the interface as a membrane between these two worlds. 'Hybrid space is conceptually different from what has been termed mixed reality, augmented reality, augmented virtuality, or virtual reality' (de Souza e Silva 2006), and for this reason encourages 'redefinition' of what physical and digital spaces actually are (2006: 273). This chimes with the work of Mitchell, which argues that information and physical spaces become inter-woven as mobile information technologies move out into the city. This has become one of the central questions informing work that attempts to understand the spatial dynamics of ICTs, or what might be called urban informatics. In this field, the interface is a key conceptual tool for rethinking connections between social and physical spaces. Interfaces are not simply conceptual devices but are also material technologies that are themselves to be subjected to critical analysis. A key aspect of such analysis is, as Manovich suggests, that they are placed in historical context, and their form and design understood in connection to those of previous technologies (see for example Sterne 2003). But this, on its own is not enough, for interfaces are also active in the social connections we make, in the cultural productions and consumptions they mediate, and in facilitating the spread of software across and through everyday spaces. In this respect, the interface is not a neutral mediator, for it shapes information and understandings in the act of translation between humans and machines. This raises, in turn, important questions of power and human agency – questions we will return to in **Chapters 7** and **8** in our consideration of interactivity and simulation.

CONCLUSION

In light of the above, of what benefit is the concept of 'interface' for the analysis of new media? This question is difficult to answer in the first instance, for this is perhaps the least developed of the concepts that we consider in this book. In place of clearly developed positions and definitions there are, for the most part, attempts to build the interface into an analysis of the boundary-dissolving potentials of new media on one hand, and the emergence of new power structures and digital divides on the other. But one common feature to both these approaches is an attempt to think increas-ingly in spatial terms about interfaces, something that might feed back into – and in turn enhance –the concept of information considered in **Chapter 3**. For treating the interface as an analytic concept enables questions to be asked of the boundaries between humans and machines, and of how information comes to be materialized in networks, cities and bodies. Such work can only proceed, however, if we start with the premise that interfaces are not just technical entities, but also conceptual devices that open up these boundaries to sociological and cultural analysis (see Beer 2008). This means treating the interface, at least in the first instance, as the 'pivot of an emerging new set of human/machine relations' (Poster 1996: 21). Interfaces are not just portals or ways into different systems, but are phenomena that play an active role in structuring the use of, and perhaps even emotional attachment to, new media technologies (see Turkle 2007). Interfaces order and facilitate information access, and enable the reproduction and consumption of culture in particular ways and in particular places. For this reason, both the conceptual underpinnings and materialities of interfaces require critical interrogation. Through such interrogation, a concept of the interface might be forged that vitalizes analysis of systems and their boundaries, and which helps us examine how these come to be mediated, materialized and perhaps recast in the everyday operation of new media technologies.

A barrier to be faced or perhaps a resource to be drawn upon in pursuing such work is the sheer complexity and range of interfaces that are to be found in everyday settings. Distinguishing between interfaces is not straightforward, particularly if they are embedded within other interfaces. This is something that we address further in considering the connection between hardware and software in **Chapter 7**. Finally, however, it is worth returning to the idea of the interface as a concept, for as stated throughout this chapter interfaces are not just technical devices but are also conceptual spaces or surfaces that mediate between different systems. These surfaces tend to be active and fast-moving, and for this reason it is possible and perhaps even necessary to think of interface as both a noun and a verb. For if it is to be a useful concept it needs to address *the* interface and also *how* things interface. It is to be a thinking technology that enables us to reflect on our constant switched-on-ness. Such a concept might help cross some of the binary oppositions that have structured new media theory to date – hardware/software, physical/virtual, conceptual/material – and which to some extent have constrained the scope for critical analysis of the new media age. The interface is that space between these apparent dualisms – a space of negotiation and a point of contact between different systems that continually needs to be explored. Interface is a concept that enables connections to be forged between the infrastructural concepts of information and networks, as described in the previous two chapters, and the more experiential concepts that are to follow.

Chapter Summary

- Interfaces place seemingly discrete systems into contact and communication with one another.
- The concept of the interface shifts the focus of media theory from network structures to the question of *how* connections between different systems, machines and bodies are made possible.
- This concept calls into question the boundaries between human and machines, hardware and software, and the virtual and material.
- New media interfaces shape communication and information access, and increasingly are sites for surveillance and power.
- Such interfaces are becoming ubiquitous in everyday life, and because of this are often taken for granted rather than subjected to critical analysis.

5 ARCHIVE

We do not live in a society that uses digital archives, we live in an information society that *is* a digital archive.

Brouwer and Mulder (2003: 6)

The primary focus of most social and cultural theories of new media, to date, has been on the ways in which they have revolutionized communication rather than on the unprecedented capacities of such media for data storage and retrieval. This focus, however, is not especially new, for – as we have seen already in **Chapter 3** – back in the late 1940s the information science of Shannon and Weaver centred on the technical means through which data is transmitted and received rather than on how it is stored or archived. Given this apparent gap, the present chapter will turn to the question of information storage, and will ask, more specifically, how archives might be conceptualized in an age of digital media. One preliminary answer might be that archives today are increasingly *networked* structures that enable the storage, retrieval and accelerated communication of unprecedented amounts of data. Such archives are material or virtual technologies that also have an underlying *conceptual* design, even if they do not always work as planned. The connection of these related aspects – the conceptual and the material and/or virtual – will lie at the heart of this chapter which will seek, above all, to question the widespread assumption that archives are depositories for the storage of written documents, and that they are 'constituted through the act of writing' (Milner 1999: 89). Against such privileging of the written form, which is prevalent in Derridean and Foucaultian approaches, it will be argued instead that archives now need to be understood in light of new media technologies that are changing the way we create, access and store information. Traditional archives made up of documents housed in an official and regulated space have not disappeared altogether – *far from it*. But they are now only a part of the story as online technologies have opened new possibilities for the remote storage of images (still and moving), sounds *and* texts which, increasingly, are accessible to the masses, not least because they require little technical knowledge to use.

This chapter will challenge traditional conceptions of the archive as a body of 'officially' classified texts by arguing instead that they are increasingly decentralized in form and are more open than ever to 'lay' access and production. This change in the structure and technology of the archive is in large part due to the wide circulation of Internet-based media, and beyond this to a transformation of the Internet itself: from a static information source to a dynamic space where anyone with a connection can, with even the most basic of computer skills, create content. This new space of the Internet, which some have called Web 2.0 (O'Reilly 2005; Beer and Burrows 2007), is characterized not only by the collaborative ventures of individual users, but also by a range of new archival phenomena or 'architectures of participation' (O'Reilly 2005) – from everyday blogging to the more creative and technical 'mashing-up' of different datasets. This new world of Web 2.0 is fast-changing and thus difficult to make sense of theoretically, but at least one thing is clear: emergent forms of online communication are developing hand in hand with new structures and capacities for the storage and archiving of information. For this reason, the present chapter argues that the concept of the archive needs to be reconsidered in the new media age. More specifically, it argues that archives need to be rethought in the light of multimedia technologies or applications that expand the possible forms they might take, and which, increasingly, place responsibility for the design and governance of archives into the hands of their users.

DERRIDA'S *ARCHIVE FEVER*

A key reference point for recent analyses of archival technologies is the work of Jacques Derrida, in particular his *Archive Fever* (1996; see Lynch 1999, Featherstone 2000, Steedman 2001). This difficult essay – originally a lecture delivered by Derrida in 1994 under the title 'The Concept of the Archive: A Freudian Impression' – is significant because it calls for a rethinking of the archive in the light of changes brought about by digital communications and storage media. The jacket cover of this book claims that it offers 'a major statement on the pervasive impact of electronic media, particularly e-mail, which threaten to transform the entire public and private space of humanity'. This promise, however, is not borne out by the actual text, which in practice is far more modest, and for the most part says very little about either e-mail or the connection between archives and new media technologies more generally. Instead, Derrida returns at length to the writings of Sigmund Freud in order to analyse, in quite abstract terms, the connection between archives and the structures of human memory (see for example Derrida 1996: 35). This might seem far removed from the concerns of a book on new media, but *Archive Fever* remains a useful theoretical resource not least because it opens with an etymological study of the concept of the archive. Derrida traces this concept to the Greek word *arkhē*, which, he explains, means both commencement and commandment. He sees this etymology as important is it binds the archive historically to government, power and law. This reading is, at surface level, close to that forwarded famously by Michel Foucault in his *Archaeology of Knowledge*: 'The archive is first the law of what can be said, the system which governs the appearance of statements as unique events' (1972: 129). But, in practice, Derrida's and Foucault's analyses follow quite different paths. For whereas Foucault's primary concern is to trace out the discursive rules that govern the different epistemes of Renaissance, classical and modern knowledge (see Foucault 1970), Derrida returns to Greek antiquity to study the *arkheion*: that home of the archive that was 'initially a house, a domicile, an address, the superior magistrates, the *archons*, those who commanded' (Derrida 1996: 2). His interest in the *arkheion* lies in the close connection it helped forge between the archive and the political power of those that governed it:

> The citizens who … held and signified political power were considered to possess the right to make or represent the law. On account of their publicly recognized authority, it is at their home, in that *place* which is their house … that official documents are filed … It is thus, in this *domiciliation*, in this house arrest, that archives take place. (Derrida 1996)

The key point of interest in this description is that the archive was originally situated in a privileged *space* (in this case, the household) over which the *archons* or magistrates traditionally governed. For Derrida, the consequence of this is that the archive became both a place of commencement and of commandment: it was both sequential and jussive. Or, in other words, an archive took place (as an event) because it could be kept in place, both physically and politically.

This 'place', however, is more complex than might at first be thought. This is because the archive worked by storing data by placing it under the control of the *archons*, and by situating it in a private space that at the same time had a degree of public access. Michael Lynch explains: 'The classical archive is in certain respects like the Cartesian mind, in that it is domiciled in a private space and controlled by a person who dwells in that space. There is one big difference, however. An archive, though guarded, is a public space' (1999: 79). This interplay of public and private space remains of contemporary interest. For whereas in Derrida's description of Greek times public (state) records were sited in privileged private locations that were governed by a select few, today the reverse is increasingly true. This is because private lives are now routinely displayed and archived in public spaces that often have free and unrestricted access and which are governed in the loosest sense by their users. This development is tied to the emergence of Internet technologies that not only enable lay-users to have unprecedented access to public data, but also to archive their own lives almost in real-time. Examples of this new situation include (auto)biographical videos posted on YouTube, or personal thoughts and photos posted on users' MySpace profiles and other social networking sites such as Facebook. These examples suggest that the archive is changing in basis, as is the relation it forges between public and private space. The private, for example a film taken in a family home of a daughter wearing her formal ball gown or 'prom dress', becomes public when posted on a site such as YouTube. While this might seem trivial, it is one instance of a broader change in the underlying social or cultural structure of the archive, which is becoming increasingly individualized. For instead of existing as public, state-governed technologies that are located in guarded private spaces, archives increasingly are public forms that are open to individual construction, maintenance and control – something we will discuss in further detail in a moment.

This takes us a long way from the work of Derrida, which focuses more on changes to human memory and the human mind that are brought about by different sets of technologies rather than on archives per se. This is clearly stated in the opening chapter (*Exergue*) of *Archive Fever*, where he poses the following question:

> Is the psychic apparatus *better represented* or is it *affected differently* by all the technical mechanisms for archivization and for reproduction, for prostheses of so-called live memory, for simulacrums of living things which already are, and will increasingly be, more refined, complicated, powerful than the 'mystic pad' (microcomputing, electronization, computerization, etc.)? (Derrida 1996: 15, emphasis in original)

It is worth pausing for a moment to reflect on what exactly is at stake in this passage. Perhaps the best place to start is with Derrida's reference to the 'mystic pad' (*der Wunderblock*) or the 'printator' – a technology seemingly far removed from today's mobile computational devices. The reference is a veiled response to Freud, who in his 1925 'Note upon the "Mystic Writing Pad"' wrote about this device – 'a slab of dark brown resin or wax with a paper edging' over which 'is laid a thin transparent sheet' – as a means for externalizing memory in technology. The mystic pad caught Freud's attention because it combined the permanence of ink on paper with the transience of chalk on slate, and so enabled both the recording and rewriting of data. This led him, in turn, to draw a parallel between this primitive technology of (re)inscription and the deeper structures of the human psyche. Freud says, for example, that 'If we imagine one hand writing upon the surface of the Mystic Writing-Pad while another periodically raises its covering sheet from the wax slab, we shall have a concrete representation of the way in which I tried to picture the functioning of the perceptual apparatus of our mind' (Freud 1991 [1925]: 212).

Derrida turns to this text by Freud because he is interested in the technical objects and structures of psychoanalysis, in particular 'the psychic apparatus as an apparatus of perception', and 'the archivization of psychoanalysis itself' (Derrida 1996: 15). This connection might well be intriguing, especially if it were to shed light on the ways in which new media technologies structure our capacity for thought and communication. Derrida's analysis, however, while opening important questions about the comparable structures of the psychic apparatus and various forms of media, says next to nothing about either the ways in which contemporary technological forms structure the human mind, or the psychoanalytic techniques and apparatuses to which such technologies have given rise. This is something that has been addressed by Jacques Lacan, particularly in his writings on the ego and cybernetics, and more recently by Friedrich Kittler, who maps Lacan's registers of symbolic, real and imaginary onto a range of different communications and storage media (see **Chapter 3** of this book, and Gane 2005a). Instead, Derrida returns to Freud in order to explore a different line of argument. He asks in the first instance what is meant by the exteriorization of memory, and following this whether contemporary 'archival machines' change or 'affect the essentials of Freud's discourse' (Derrida 1996: 15). His answer to these questions is brief and is drawn from one of his earlier texts, *Writing and Difference* (2001; in French 1967), in which he chides Freud for not looking at the possibility of machines simulating or 'resembling' memory, and for focusing on the Mystic Pad rather than more advanced storage media of his day. Derrida extends this critique in *Archive Fever*, where he remarks of the Mystic Pad that 'compared to other machines for storing archives, it is a child's toy' (1996: 14). He also objects to Freud's failure to question the changes that advancements in media technology brought to the psychic apparatus, as well as culture more generally. In a key passage he protests that

> the technical structure of the *archiving archive* also determines the structure of the *archivable* content even in its relationship to the future. The archivization produces as much as it records the event. This is also our political experience of the so-called news media. This means that, *in the past*, psychoanalysis would not have been what it was … if Email, for example, had existed. And *in the future* it will no longer be what Freud and so many psychoanalysts have anticipated, from the moment E-mail, for example, became possible. (Derrida 1996: 17)

The main thrust of this passage is that media technologies are not passive conveyors of content or representations, but actively structure archives and perhaps even their users. Derrida here appears to fall into line with McLuhan (1964), who famously proclaims that the medium is the message, by which is meant that media structure the content of the messages they communicate, along with the basis of human culture more generally.

The problem for Derrida is that he falls foul of his own argument. For to understand the current connection between media technologies and the content they circulate, or the connection between archives and the data they store or memories they produce, knowledge of contemporary archiving technologies is needed, along with some technical understanding of the ways in which such technologies produce their effects (which are not always intended). Derrida, however, appears to lack any such understanding or interest. Curiously, he focuses on one technology, e-mail, which, he says, is 'privileged in my opinion ... because electronic mail even more than the fax, is on the way to transforming the entire public and private space of humanity, and first of all the limit between private, the secret (private and public), and the public or the phenomenal' (1996: 17). But in privileging e-mail as *the* contemporary archival medium, Derrida repeats Freud's error in focusing on the primitive technology of the Mystic Pad in an age marked by the birth of the film, phonograph and gramophone. For in 1995, when Derrida delivered the lecture which was to become *Archive Fever*, e-mail was only one technology of many that made up the multi-media world of the Internet. Indeed, the Internet at this point in time existed, albeit in a more primitive incarnation, as a hypertextual archive of words, images and sounds (often rolled together in the same environment) as well as data, code or information, which are never simply discursive in form (see Kittler 1986: 157). Given this, why does Derrida privilege e-mail in *Archive Fever*? Why does he limit the archive to the communication and storage of discursive forms? The answer is perhaps that there is a textual bias to Derrida's position that privileges writing (in this case in the form of an e-mail) over all other forms of archival data. Derrida thus ends up taking a comparable position to that of Foucault, whose analysis of archival technologies stretches only to around 1850, the very point at which, ironically, the sovereignty of writing over data storage and transmission started to fade (a point observed by Friedrich Kittler 1990: 369–74 in his 'Afterword' to *Discourse Networks*, but missed by Manuel DeLanda 2003:8–13 in his brief analysis of the archive before and after Foucault). This means that both Derrida and Foucault share a very restricted view of what archives are, the data they store and the technologies through which they operate. By way of response, what is needed is a vision of the archive that does not start or finish with the written word, but which sees it instead as a much broader medium for the storage of data that can take many different forms. As stated above, this means considering the multimedia possibilities (sound, text and image) of new media technologies, along with the unofficial archival forms that are emerging through their use.

ARCHIVES OF THE EVERYDAY

The challenge is to rethink archives against the backdrop of increasingly sophistic-ated user-generated media applications, many of which now exist online. This task has been attempted by Arjun Appadurai, who considers the ways in which such applications are introducing a heightened 'capability of interactive users to more easily enter and edit the archive', and, following this, a tendency 'for the archive itself to be expanded by the nature and distribution of its users' (2003: 17). One approach here might be to think of the Internet as *the* unrivalled meta-archive of the contemporary world, insofar as it represents an unbounded space in which archives become tagged and potentially hyperlinked with one another (thereby giving rise to what some have called 'folksonomies', O'Reilly 2005). But care must be taken in forwarding such a position, for the Internet itself has a complex architecture and is made up of many different archival technologies, not all of which are publicly or freely accessible. (See the final section of this chapter.) This said, however, there are many online technologies that *are* open to public use, and which work to decentre or *unbind* the archive so that anyone with a connection can consume, contribute to and, to some extent, police its space. The archives that emerge as a result are, to use the words of Michael Lynch, 'popular' in form. He explains:

> A web site may be difficult to visit for persons who do not possess or have access to the requisite technology and skills, but together with other forms of elec-tronic media it has the potential to turn a body of documentary evidence into a 'popular archive' subjected to mass visitation, reproduction and dissemination. (1999: 75–6)

There are many examples of precisely this process. These might include websites such as Flickr or YouTube which contain archives of photographs or video-clips, and which gain in notoriety as they circulate around the Net, sometimes even attracting the attention of the popular press. In these user-generated archives the everyday takes on a new significance, for users post their own content and connect to others through a hyperlinked system of keywords or meta-tags, thereby enabling search and retrieval as well as browsing between connected content. This signals a basic shift in the form of the archive, which may now include sources such as hand-held mobile phone videos, web-cam blogs, sound recordings, digital photos and home video shots, thereby extending 'the walls of the archive to place it around the everyday, the world' (Featherstone 2000: 161). A key consequence of this development is that the mundane and routine find their way into the digitalized archive as people record and share their day-to-day lives, along with their personal preferences, political and religious viewpoints, and reflections on events almost as soon as they take place (Beer 2006).

This shift toward the mass archiving of the everyday is part of a wider social and cultural process that Zygmunt Bauman (see 2000, 2001b; Gane 2004: 17–46) calls *individualization*. This process involves the flow of the private interests of the household (the *oikos*) into public space (the *ecclesia*) as well as the *agora* (the classical meeting place of private and public issues). For Bauman, this is a worrying development that brings with it the trivialization of public spaces and politics, along with the reduction of citizens (which he sees as being collectively minded) to consumers (who pursue their own individual wants and desires). This position is in many ways comparable to that of Castells (see **Chapter 2**), who characterizes the new media age in terms of a shift from close-knit communal forms to me-centred networks. Andrew Keen takes a similar although more aggressive stance. In *The Cult of the Amateur*, he characterizes the new world of Web 2.0 as a mix of 'ignorance meets egoism meets bad taste meets mob rule' (Keen 2007: 1). For Keen, the user-generated world of Web 2.0 threatens to bring an end to 'informed citizenship' by blurring traditional distinctions between lay users and 'experts', and, more generally, by introducing a frivolous and narcissistic culture of the individual. He cites the website YouTube as a prime example: 'YouTube eclipses even ... blogs in the inanity and absurdity of its content. Nothing seems too prosaic or narcissistic for these videographer monkeys. The site is an infinite gallery of amateur movies showing poor fools dancing, singing, eating, washing, shopping, driving, cleaning, sleeping, or just staring into their computers' (Keen 2007: 5). For Keen, websites such as these are simply 'killing our culture'.

In our view, this is an overly negative account of the social and cultural dynamics of network society and of Web 2.0, and one that is conservative and nostalgic in its praise of the culture industry of the mid- to late twentieth century. Keen declares, for example, that with the emergence of Web 2.0 we can '[s]ay good-bye to today's experts and cultural gatekeepers – our reporters, news anchors, editors, music companies, and Hollywood movie studios. In today's cult of the amateur, the monkeys are running the show (Keen 2007:9). This passage is revealing, as it points to those aspects of modern culture that Keen treats as sacred: television, the music industry, and that icon of cultural capitalism, Hollywood. What concerns us in the present chapter, however, is what Keen's work might bring to a theory of the archive. Contrary to Keen, we would suggest that the Internet is not simply a playground for self-publicizing individuals, for potentially it is also a site for new virtual communities and perhaps even the emergence of an 'electronic agora': a virtual space in collective solutions can be sought to seemingly personal and private problems. For while archives have become increasingly individualized, this does not mean that these public spaces have become simply 'me-centred', as Bauman, Castells and, in a different way, Keen suggest. For while there are countless archives of personal photos, videos and blogs across websites such as YouTube, MySpace and Facebook, there are also striking attempts at collective collaboration between individuals for the apparent good of the whole. These might include, for example, medical support groups and information networks set up online by or for sufferers of, among other things, cancer, diabetes or heart disease.

A quite different example, and one that is hotly contested, is Wikipedia – the online encyclopaedia founded 'on the unlikely notion that an entry can be added by any web user, and edited by any other' (O'Reilly 2005). At surface level, Wikipedia would seem to be an instance of what O'Reilly calls 'collective intelligence' (2005), whereby the hyperlinked architecture of the Web is put to work for a collective purpose by individual users (known as 'wikizens'). Not everyone, however, sees this enterprise in such a positive light. Andrew Keen, for example, is deeply critical of Wikipedia, for he laments the absence of expert gatekeepers to police such archives, and comments that 'fully democratic open-source networks inevitably get corrupted by loonies' (2007: 186). Again, we would argue that this is too negative a view, not least because it downplays the work of thousands of genuine 'wikizens' who have provided knowledge (which is often quite accurate and detailed) for the use of others, and who have spent time policing inaccurate entries. What is interesting about such activity is that it blurs many of the boundaries that are common to traditional forms of sociological analysis – including many of those drawn by Bauman, Castells and even Keen. For such sharing of information and expertise is simultaneously an act of production and consumption, giving rise to what George Ritzer (2007) has recently called 'prosumer' culture. Furthermore, such activity crosses boundaries between the public and the private, and proceeds through collective efforts of a network of individualized users. In this way, such archives are the product both of the network and the individual, and for this reason, among others, we would argue that it is incorrect to claim, as do Bauman and Castells, that the network society is solely 'me-centred' in orientation, or that the world of Web 2.0 is simply frivolous and banal.

One of the most interesting features of the Internet today is that it is a space which continues to rub against public or state powers for control over information, or in Derrida's terms the authority of the *archons* (even if such powers are making something of a return; see Lessig 2006). An important development has been the emergence of file-sharing technologies (for example, BitTorrent) that elude traditional forms of government, for they enable users to connect to each other through remote technologies that bypass centralized points of control. O'Reilly explains that

> BitTorrent, like other pioneers in the P2P movement, takes a radical approach
> to internet decentralization. Every client is also a server; files are broken up into
> fragments that can be served from multiple locations, transparently harnessing

the network of downloaders to provide both bandwidth and data to other users. (2005)

The result is an archival technology that, at least in theory, takes the form of an open system. The same might be said of the interactive world of Web 2.0 which, for the most part, is defined by open and collaborative projects in which users become responsible for generating and policing content as well as consuming it (Beer 2006). The key aspect of this new world is that the archive becomes a shared project – one that includes activities, for example, such as the digitalization of music collections for others to download, the tagging of photographs and online albums or more serious individual contributions to collective projects such as Wikipedia (see above).

This situation is quite different from the vision of the archive portrayed by thinkers such as Derrida and Foucault, who tend to see it as a closed system in which texts are stored under the control of institutional or state-centred powers. Today, by contrast, archives, while to some extent still the product of collective work, are increasingly individualized and decentred. Arjun Appadurai describes this shift as follows:

> through personal websites, digital archives for all sorts of collectivities (both paid and free), storage sites in cyberspace for large data sets, and the possibility of sending pictures, sounds and text to multiple users with high speed and large amounts of high quality information, the archive is gradually freed of the orbit of the state and its official networks. (2003:17)

This shift away from state control opens up archives to a wider population of users, and to an increasingly broad range of publicly accessible materials, be these personal, commercial, state or 'intellectual' in form (the boundaries between which are no longer always clear). This, in turn, gives rise to heightened conflicts over the ownership of information, for it is not always apparent where and to whom data belong. This problem becomes particularly acute following the emergence of new media technologies that enable the accelerated communication of information, along with the ability for lay-users to 'mash' it into creative new forms. In the world of Web 2.0, notions of property and ownership become ever harder to define, let alone uphold. Andrew Keen is again critical of this development, and objects to this new age in which 'anyone, with the click of a mouse, can cut and paste content and make it their own' (2007: 143), arguing that it results in 'moral disorder'. He complains that

> Web 2.0 technology is confusing the very concept of ownership, creating a generation of plagiarists and copyright thieves with little respect for intellectual property … The digital revolution is creating a generation of cut-and-paste burglars who view all content on the Internet as common property. (2007)

But for others, including Lessig (2004), the idea of a 'free culture' or creative commons is to be welcomed precisely because it liberates information from the dynamics of the capitalist market and/or state control. In this view, the underlying morality of Web 2.0 lies in its ability to open up the archive to public access, use and design through the sharing of technical resources and know-how. This has led to the emergence of archives from below: user-generated archives that perhaps do not carry the same weight as conventional state-governed archives, but which instead document 'everyday' (Featherstone 2000) or 'ordinary' (Osborne 1999) lives at ground level while at the same time rendering them accessible to a potentially global audience. User-generated archives may thus prove to be a rich source of qualitative data for social scientists wanting to study contemporary cultural change (see Beer and Burrows 2007). Indeed, many now use the Internet as a site and a tool for 'virtual' or 'digital' ethnographic research (see Hine 2000; Dicks et al. 2005).

ARCHIVES AND MEMORY

In the above section, we outline a vision of Internet-based archives that enable mass storage of, and easy access to, data in the form of images, sounds and texts – archives which tend to work through the collaborative acts of individuals. A further but related aspect of such archives is that they forge a new connection between the archive and popular memory. Arjun Appadurai theorizes this development as follows:

> the relation of collective memory to the archive may be seen as evolving two opposed faces. On the one hand, the newer forms of electronic archiving restore the deep link of the archive to the popular memory and its practices, returning to the non-official actor the capability to choose the way in which traces and documents shall be formed into archives, whether at the level of the family, the neighbourhood, the community or other sorts of groupings outside the demography of the state. On the other hand, the electronic archive, by allowing the formation of new prosthetic socialities, denaturalises the relationship of memory and the archive, making the (interactive) archive the basis of collective memory as the substrate which guarantees the ethical value of the archive. We are thus entering an era in which the collective memory and the archive have mutually formative possibilities, thus allowing new traffic across the gap between the internalities and externalities of collective memory. (2003: 18)

There are, then, two main developments for Appadurai. First, as has been described in the opening sections of this chapter, the archive has been to some extent democratized, for the 'non-official actor' is now able to access and create online archives in ways previously unimaginable. Second, and as a result of this development, the connection between human memory and the archive is being 'denaturalized'.

Put simply, this means that the structure of human memory is changing in form because of the unprecedented powers of new media machines for data storage, and because of the near ubiquity of these machines in everyday life. This returns us to the question Derrida poses in *Archive Fever* concerning the connection of the archive (and its media) to the human psyche. For today, user-generated archives of photographs, music, videos and texts are literally everywhere, and while taking up less physical space in our lives are at the same time structuring our personal memories and identities to an ever greater extent. (For an illustrative example see Susan Yee's vignette on design and the archive in Turkle 2007.) It might even be argued that life today is increasingly being played out *through* the archive rather than simply stored within it. Indeed, it is no exaggeration to state that the storage capacities of new media archives are changing the basic fabric of contemporary social life and culture. This is implicit in Mike Featherstone's vision of the new media archive as 'a city of data ... of vast databases containing all culture's deposited wealth, where every document is potentially available, every recording playable and every picture viewable' (2000: 165–6). Appadurai, meanwhile, talks of Internet-based archives as prostheses of individuals' private existence. For him, such archives extend our lives into public space, and in so doing, expand our capacity for collective memory. This development again has complex consequences, for it gives rise to a culture that creates and stores innumerable traces of itself, and from which nothing is easily excluded (reversing the logic of previous archival forms) – for better or worse.

This has prompted a renewed interest in analysing the connections between the archive, memory and history (see for example Caygill 1999, Damasio 2003). Abdelmajid Hannoum, for example, reflects that

Case Study: Tagging and Tag Clouds

In the closing sections of this chapter we look at Web 2.0 and the emergence of user-generated online archives. A key point of interest in this discussion is the way in which such archives are organized and structured through processes of *tagging*. The user-generated content of Web 2.0 — photographs on Flickr or video clips on YouTube — is made up of data (photos or videos) that are posted by the user, but also of metadata: information or tags that are connected to these posts and which enable them to be

classified, archived and searched. Tagging promotes the connectivity of information within and in some cases between new media archives. It is one practice among many that transforms the archive into a networked storage medium by making connections between vast amounts of data at unprecedented speeds. Such networked archives revolutionize everyday practices of data storage and retrieval. Tagging a photo on Flickr with the word 'York', for example, means that anyone searching for York on Flickr can, with the minimum of

To say archive is to refer not only to the masses of witnessing, but also to a place, a physical and social space. The place is where both the inclusion and exclusion of discourses happen that provide the framework for the historiographic operation. This is the domain not of history or historiography, but rather of a distinct discipline called *archiving*. (2005: 128)

What is important in this statement is less Hannoum's restricted focus, like that of Foucault, on discourse, but rather the idea that archiving is related to yet clearly distinct from history. Whereas archives gather and record data, history sketches out narratives and links together selected parts of the archive into what might be called knowledge. For Hannoum, archives in themselves are made up 'of a multiplicity of sources, voices', and can be described as 'polyphonic' (2005). This idea of a *polyphonic archive* is particularly appropriate given the emergence of Web 2.0 applications that assemble a multiplicity of voices and data in the form of audio, visual and text files. These user-generated online archives take the idea of polyphony to new extremes, even to the point where – in the case of technologies such as Wikipedia – competing voices can edit and potentially erase the contributions of one another.

One question this poses is of the form of historical memory to which new media archives now give rise. The difficulty is that online user-generated archives are quite different to traditional paper-based archives, for they work through practices of browsing, hyperlinking and tagging, along with more conventional techniques of accumulating data. These new archives, in the words of Mike Featherstone, 'facilitate ... multiple entry points and non-linear associational jumps across the material' (2000: 173). This means that pathways through them need not follow a

---

effort, locate that photo and other photos with the same tag. Perhaps surprisingly, there is currently little work in media or cultural studies that addresses such practices and processes of tagging. However, as Web 2.0 archives become increasingly ubiquitous we will be pressed to understand how tagging operates, how it shapes online practices, and how it impacts upon the data that we store and retrieve. A good place to start might be the analysis of tag clouds. Tag clouds are simply a visualization of the tags connected with a particular piece of content, or a visualization of the most popular tags on a website. These tags are formed into a cloud formation with the most frequently selected tags written in larger and bolder lettering. Tag clouds, then, are meta-informational forms. Analysis of such forms is needed in order to pursue an understanding of the social and cultural consequences of tagging, and, more broadly, of the ways in which new media archives structure access to, and the communication of, information.

predetermined or even logical order but can be forged in the very act of using them. Featherstone explains that

> A key aspect of the electronic search and research process is the use of hypertext. In contrast to the ideal of memory as a store into which one descends to pull things out, hypertext works on a less hierarchical more lateral view of knowledge as the links between data. (Featherstone 2000: 175)

This type of multi-dimensional navigation remains at the heart of new media archives today and, as Featherstone suggests, forges a new model of memory that works through linkages rather than hierarchical constraints. This connection between memory and the archive has been addressed by Howard Caygill, who observes that '[t]he elision of the work of memory with a technique for retrieving information from an archive is intrinsic to the western art of memory' (1999: 1). For Caygill, the tension present at the heart of the Web is between memory as invention and as recollection, a tension which he traces as far back as Plato's *Meno*. Caygill, however, is less positive than Featherstone about the potential of Web-based memory, for he argues that the 'interoperability' and commerciality of the Web has sacrificed the most inventive aspects of hypertext, and has in turn reduced the Web into 'an archival system of retrieval of information from an existing stock' (Caygill 1999: 9). It is debateable whether Web 2.0, with its creative user-generated data, can be seen in the same way. But one thing that is clear: changes in the form of the Internet alter in turn the basic structure of the archive (see Brouwer and Mulder 2003), and with this the basis and content of collective memory. For as Featherstone observes, 'shifts in archival technology … change the form within which culture is recorded', and in so doing change the very conditions under which 'culture is produced and enacted' (2000: 180).

This raises, in turn, important questions concerning the connection of the archive to history, and of the power relationships that are embedded within and also emerge out of this connection. The key figure to have addressed such questions is Michel Foucault. Foucault's interest in archives is primarily a political one, for he seeks to expose the laws through which certain 'official' bodies of historical knowledge are admitted to archives, while other 'subjugated' knowledges are excluded and subsequently erased from memory. Foucault, in short, sees archives as sites of inclusion and exclusion through which historical memory is governed. But is this still the case in a new media age in which archives have become individualized and opened, increasingly, to public use and design? This question is complex, but one answer is that issues of power/knowledge and inclusion/exclusion are equally important in considering archives today but for a different reason: they are no longer sites for the centralized control of historical material but are structured instead by new inequalities of access both to and through information communication technologies. For as archives have become increasingly individualized, the problem is not so much that of knowledge or data which might be included or excluded from archives, but rather that of the types of access users have to different archiving technologies or databases.

This question of access is important for it shifts attention to the underlying power structures and inequalities of the new media age (see for example Loader 1998, Loader and Keeble 2004, O'Hara and Stevens 2006). The most basic of these inequalities is the digital division between those who have access to the physical technologies needed to take part in the online world (computers and broadband networks) from those who do not. However, as computer-based technologies have become increasingly ubiquitous (at least in the Western world) this divide has become less acute, and attention has shifted to the type and speed of access users have, along with the training they need in order to gain the most from the technologies at hand. This has given rise to more nuanced conceptions of the 'digital divide' which also look at the way that new media technologies can be employed to sort and classify their users (see for example Nettleton et al. 2005, Turow 2006, Bowker and Star 1999). Coupled with this are questions regarding access to archival data itself. For while popular archives such as Facebook or MySpace tend to offer individuals free usage (albeit in return for the information we give up about ourselves) there are other commercial archives or databases (for example, financial websites such as ADVFN or MoneyAM) that charge for different levels of access according to the type of data that is sought. New media archives are thus by no means immune to the dynamics of the capitalist marketplace (something we consider at greater length in our analysis of Web 2.0 in the following chapter). Further examples of this include Internet search engines that provide free access to end users but do so by ordering search results according to those that have paid for a premium position. This development again reflects the movement of the archive out of state hands and into the individualized world of contemporary market capitalism, which is governed by algorithms that organize and structure online content (see Lash 2007). Notably, this connection between the archive and capitalist culture is absent in the writings of Foucault and Derrida, for whom the archive remained tied to the powers of the state legislators or *arkons*. This situation, however, has now changed, and because of this demands detailed re-evaluation – something that is beyond the scope of the present work.

CONCLUSION

The argument of this chapter is that archives are no longer housed simply in buildings such as libraries and museums, but are now increasingly generated and maintained by lay users in virtual environments. For this reason, it is necessary to reconsider the archive, particularly in the light of Web 2.0 applications such as YouTube, Wikipedia or Facebook that *unbind* the archive from its institutional context and from its traditional concern for textual data. This is a key shift, for as Mike Featherstone states, with 'the digital archive we see a move away from the concept of the archive as a physical place to store records ... to that of the archive as a virtual site facilitating immediate transfer' (Featherstone 2006: 595). New media archives are multimedia devices that are composed of audio and visual data as well as text, and work increasingly through open access software that encourages user participation. They are also material and/or virtual devices for the storage of data that have an underlying conceptual design that in many ways reflects broader changes in contemporary society and culture. In part, this is because archives contain traces of the practices and tastes of their users, while at the same time saying something about the deeper structures and dynamics of everyday life. New media archives are individualized *and* highly collaborative, and are sites for the emergence of new forms of popular memory which operate through the storage of everyday and quite ordinary phenomena. They are also potential sites for the emergence of new forms of power, and, more particularly, for new configurations of power/information that in many ways take us beyond Foucauldian ideas of power/knowledge. For this reason, it is important that new media archives are analysed in the light of the dynamics of contemporary capitalism and in connection to the hierarchies of access to which these give rise.

Chapter Summary

- By focusing on the archive we draw attention to the ways in which information is *stored*.
- The writings of Jacques Derrida and Michel Foucault on the archive are now outdated as they focus primarily on the storage of written texts.
- Archives, increasingly, are multimedia devices that can store a wide-range of data, including numbers, texts, images, video and sound.
- There is a trend toward the individualization of archives as personal lives are being documented and displayed in publicly accessible spaces.
- Responsibility for the governance of new media archives lies increasingly with their users.

6 INTERACTIVITY

Interactivity is one of the most frequently used concepts in new media theory. It is often invoked as a benchmark for differentiating 'new' digital media from 'older' analogue forms, and for this reason it is not unusual to find new media referred to as *interactive* media. But herein lies a problem: in spite of the almost ubiquitous presence of this concept in commentaries on new media it is not always clear what makes media interactive or what is meant exactly by the term interactivity. Interactivity is a concept that tends to be used to bypass descriptions of the workings of media technologies, and as a result all too often escapes sustained analytical and critical attention. Tanjev Schultz has responded to this situation by suggesting that the 'term is so inflated now that one begins to suspect that there is much less to it than some people want to make it appear' (2000: 205). The argument of the present chapter, however, is precisely the reverse: that there is more to the concept of interactivity than one might think. We will attempt to show this by looking at the work of a number of recent commentators, including Stephen Graham, Lev Manovich and Spiro Kiousis, who together give an idea of what the term interactivity might mean in different disciplinary settings, and how it might be put to work as a concept. Our basic argument is that interactivity is a useful concept for the analysis of new media, in particular for the consideration of political aspects of user-generated online content (see **Chapter 5**), as long as it is deployed with precision. This is particularly important in an age in which new media are commonly marketed as interactive, and are lauded for their potential for facilitating new social and cultural activities. If we are not careful, such rhetoric can easily seep into academic discourse, with the consequence that interactivity is left as an unexplained entity, or as something that is taken to be self-evident when in fact this is far from the case.

The aim of the present chapter, then, is to place the concept of interactivity under critical scrutiny. One thinker who has done just this is Lev Manovich (2001), who offers a complex typology of interactivity based on a theory of the 'remediation' or historical entwining of different media technologies (see **Chapter 4** for a discussion of this in relation to the concept of interface; see also Bolter and Grusin 1999). In the light of such work, this chapter will reassess what is meant by the term interactivity. First, we will attempt to move beyond utopian visions of technology that see inter-active media as freeing us from the limits of geographical and bodily spaces – what Stephen Graham (2004) calls the 'dream of transcendence' and Manovich (2001) the 'myth of interactivity'. Second, we will look more generally at recent social theor-ies of media interactivity, in particular those that have attempted to repoliticize this concept by applying it to the study of communication, memory and notions of active citizenship. Finally, we will explore emergent forms of interactivity by analysing examples of web applications that encourage the production of user-generated content. (See also the analysis of the archive in **Chapter 5**.) This development is important for it raises a host of sociological and political questions about the connection of 'interactive' media to new forms of intelligent or 'knowing' capitalism that feed on the information we give up about ourselves when we go online.

THE MYTH OF INTERACTIVITY?

In advertisements for new technologies it is commonplace to see and hear slogans telling us of the new-found functionality of digital media, and of how their 'interactivity' can enhance our working lives or leisure time (see Beer 2008). Nigel Thrift (2005: 20–50) has described this in terms of a cultural turn in the business sector whereby capitalist organizations attempt to theorize their own products. Such rhetoric is also part of a wider discourse of digital enlightenment in which machines are seen to be increasingly 'intelligent' and, with this, able to bring new freedoms for their users. Woolgar (2002) observes that such hyperbole or 'cyberbole' was widespread in the early 1990s, when many viewed the Internet as a technology that promised unimagined and unhindered opportunities for creative action and sociality. Against this backdrop, interactivity became a concept that could easily be sold. Graeme Kirkpatrick reflects that in 'the mid-1990s, interactivity was a kind of buzzword, used by the computer industry to hype up the new wave of computer technology' (Kirkpatrick 2004: 129; see also Schultz 2000: 205). The power of such technology was that it claimed to give users an 'interactive' experience, often by enabling them to mould media to suit their individual preferences (or, at least, this was the perception and their selling point). Today, this is taken a step further with the emergence of increasingly mobile devices that promise liberation from the physical constraints of communication. Stephen Graham (2004) calls this the 'anything-anywhere-anytime dream' in which the promise of interactivity is that it will deliver smooth and unlimited *inter*-action between users and machines in practically any setting. Graham argues that while this has happened to some extent, the envisioned transcendence of bodies or of physical geography has not been realized. Instead, we have witnessed something less spectacular and more mundane as digital technologies have become integral parts of our everyday lives, and have been 'remediated' into everyday spaces and places, including the workplace and the home (between which there is often no longer any clear distinction).

Graham's position is that there is no straightforward movement toward heightened interactivity in the new media age, for rather we are 'experiencing a complex and infinitely diverse range of transformations where new and old practices and media technologies become mutually linked and fused in an ongoing blizzard of change' (Graham 2004: 11). Understanding interactivity – along with many of the other concepts addressed in this book – against this backdrop is no easy task. One way of doing so might be to follow Graham in moving away from interactivity as a transcendent ideal or dream and instead to forge a concept of interactivity through an analysis of the workings of new media in everyday life. This is something that we consider further in the final section of this chapter. We also dig beneath the 'cyberbole' of the new media age by considering the power structures embedded in digital technologies that structure the actions of users while at the same time giving the impression of interactivity. This question of the connection between interactivity and power or agency will be addressed in detail in our analysis of simulation in **Chapter 7**. But first, in the present chapter, we consider the concept of interactivity through the lens of media history, and ask whether interactivity is something that emerges with the digital age, or whether it has a longer and more complex history throughout which it assumes different forms. ·

One thinker to have addressed such questions in detail is Lev Manovich. (See also **Chapter 4** on the concept of interface, and Bolter and Grusin 1999 for an alternative account.) Manovich adopts a genealogical method of media analysis, one designed to 'analyze the language of new media by placing it within the history of modern visual and media cultures' and to ask, above all, of 'the ways in which new media relies on older cultural forms and languages' and 'the ways in which it breaks with them' (2001: 8). His message is clear: many of the 'allegedly unique' principles of new media can be found in early forms of cinema, even if cinema itself has now been transformed by a process of computerization. Digital media are thus seen as nothing essentially new, for the elements that make up these media are to be found, if only in essence, in earlier cultural forms. Manovich's stance here is similar to that of Stephen Graham's, as it moves away from the idea that new media breaks from the past through its promise of heightened interactivity and 'transcendence' of previous bodily and social limitations. But Manovich goes a step further by drawing into question the very idea that new media are interactive. In a chapter dedicated to interactivity in *The Language of New Media*, he declares: 'As with *digital* I avoid using *interactive* in this book without qualifying it, for the same reason – I find the concept to be too broad to be truly useful' (Manovich 2001: 55). In the first instance, Manovich sees interactivity as too loose a term to assist us in the analysis of contemporary media. However, he also forwards a deeper argument, namely that the supposed interactivity of the digital age is a myth because new media technologies are often no more interactive than their analogue counterparts (pp. 55–62; see also **Chapter 4**). In forwarding this argument, Manovich takes a quite different position to that of Marshall McLuhan and his many followers, for whom electric technologies promote or rather demand greater interactivity. It is instructive to pause for a moment to consider the differences between the approaches of McLuhan and Manovich, for both address the different types of interactivity that arise from various media, and in so doing help us address the concept of interactivity in more theoretical terms.

Recent debates about the interactivity of media can, in many ways, be traced back to the writings of McLuhan. McLuhan's basic position is that 'traditional' media such as books and films (which he treats together; see McLuhan 1964: 312) are 'interactive' insofar as they demand the reader or viewer to create some kind of mental accompaniment to their content. These media are 'hot' because, like other media such as the radio, they extend a single one of our senses in 'high definition'. But with the advent of television, he argues, things change, for this medium broadcasts a 'mosaic image' that can never extend any one of our senses to the same degree. In an age in which television has become a home cinema, this argument now seems outdated, as does the idea that interactivity involves the extension of a single sense to a high degree. For why focus on a single sense, and what, exactly, is to count as 'high' definition? Such difficulties riddle McLuhan's work, but his position remains intriguing nonetheless. He argues that television, as with all other 'cool media', demands a higher level of audience participation, or what we might call interaction, as they leave more to be 'filled in' by the audience. This leads him to declare that 'Hot media are ... low in participation, and cool media are high in participation by the audience' (McLuhan 1964: 24–5). This is because, in his view, books and films, which demand some degree of mental interaction with the medium, supply one of our senses with more information than cooler media such as the television and telephone, which require us to 'fill in' more. Cool media tend to call for a different type of interaction, one centred on oral dialogue rather than the construction of a accompaniment in one's head. (The telephone is a good example here – see McLuhan 1964: 289–99.) This is why, for McLuhan (although he is probably alone here), 'It is not pleasant to turn on TV just for oneself in a hotel room, nor even at home. The TV mosaic demands social completion and dialogue' (McLuhan 1964: 319).

For Manovich, things are quite different. Whereas for McLuhan media such as books and cinema are not truly interactive, for Manovich quite the reverse is true: they are more interactive (higher in participation) than digital media forms precisely because they demand us to create a mental accompaniment. Manovich, to a much greater extent than McLuhan, sees media such as painting, books and cinema as succeeding by depriving our senses of high-level or complete information. They work because they demand us to fill in gaps in visual or audio narratives, and to construct our own readings, images or even dialogues through interaction with the medium in question. In other words, non-electronic media are far cooler than McLuhan supposed, for they tend to be 'interactive' by definition. Manovich gives the example of classical and modern art:

> Ellipses in literary narration, missing details of objects in visual art, and other representational 'shortcuts' require the user to fill in missing information. Theatre and painting also rely on techniques of staging and composition to orchestrate the viewer's attention over time, requiring her to focus on different parts of the display. (2001: 56)

Even sculpture and architecture might be seen as interactive media, for they demand the viewer 'to move her whole body to experience the spatial structure' (2001: 56). The same might be said of those media forms that, for McLuhan, are really 'hot', such as cinema. Cinema is particularly important for Manovich because, he claims, it is 'the key cultural form of the twentieth century', and as such it serves as the 'conceptual lens' through which he analyses recent changes in media technologies (2001: 9). Again, with cinema, we find an argument for the interactivity of 'older' media forms:

> Beginning in the 1920s, new narrative techniques such as film montage forced audiences to bridge quickly the mental gaps between unrelated images. Film cinematography actively guided the viewer to switch from one part of a frame to another. The new representational style of semi-abstraction, which along with photography became the 'international style' of modern visual culture, required the viewer to reconstruct represented objects from a bare minimum – a few patches of colour, shadows cast by the objects not represented directly. (Manovich 2001: 56)

Contrary to McLuhan, Manovich argues that cinema is not only highly interactive as a medium, but, even in its classical form, is low rather than high in sensual 'definition', meaning that, according to McLuhan's classification of internal media structures, it is a 'cool' rather than 'hot' media technology.

What we get in the work of Manovich is a reversal of McLuhan's basic position, and with this a different theory of media interactivity. Whereas for McLuhan electronic media are cooler than analogue media, since in general they are not 'well filled with data' and are thus more interactive. For Manovich, forms such as cinema and books operate by depriving our senses of certain data and are therefore interactive by definition. In fact, for Manovich, media such as cinema are *more* interactive than so-called 'interactive' digital media (even those based upon oral dialogue), for they demand us to fill in more, meaning that computerized culture, to use McLuhan's typology, is becoming hotter rather than cooler. A key reason for this is that while new media give the appearance of being highly interactive they often offer something far more restricted: a limited number of preprogrammed options that in turn structure our usage. (Digital television might be one example.) Such media are interactive but only in a limited way, for rather than really engaging us for the most part they prompt us to select from menus or follow predefined pathways. (Many video games work in this way.) For Manovich, this means a fall from the past, for we now rarely create our own thought but all-too-often merely select from rigid menus or branching structures that have been created by someone else.

Manovich warns, as a consequence, that the term 'interactive' must be used with a degree of caution. In *The Language of New Media*, he argues that modern HCI [Human Computer Interfaces] enable real-time manipulation of data and are therefore 'interactive' in a *different* way to that of other media (not simply more or less so). In view of this, he suggests that we be more precise by distinguishing between types of interactive structures. In particular, he proposes that we replace the broad idea of computer interactivity with a range of more specific definitions, including 'menu-based interactivity, scalability, simulation, image-interface, and image-instrument' (Manovich 2001: 56), for these definitions, in turn, allow computer-based media to be contrasted to earlier interactive forms, and in so doing place the concept of interactivity itself into question. Moreover, Manovich formulates a series of *interactivity types* that are either 'closed' or 'open' in form. Examples of 'closed' interactivity, he argues, include *branching-tree interactivity* (sometimes called menu-based interactivity), which operates as follows:

> When the user reaches a particular object, the program presents her with choices and allows her to choose among them. Depending on the value chosen the user advances along a particular branch of the tree. In this case the information used by a program is the output of the user's cognitive process. (2001: 38)

The key feature of branching-tree interactivity is that choices tend to be made by users from a set of predetermined options. It is thus a semi-closed form. Manovich continues:

> This is the simplest kind of interactivity; more complex kinds are also possible in which both the elements and the structure of the whole object are either modified or generated on the fly in response to the user's interaction with a program. We can refer to such implementations as *open interactivity* to distinguish them from

the *closed interactivity* that uses fixed elements arranged in a fixed branching structure. (2001: 40; emphasis in original)

This passage illustrates the difference between open and closed interactivity. On one hand, responsive, complex and flexible systems provide users with a broad range of 'open' possibilities that themselves might be open to definition. On the other, closed systems allow users to choose from a limited set of strictly defined pathways. Interactivity hence might be thought of as operating at different scales, with systems located along an open/closed axis according to how open their basic structures are to user design and change. The concept of interactivity here provides a useful point of entry into debates about the nature of our engagements with the technical infrastructures of new media technologies, and the extent to which these infrastructures shape our usage of new media. This is something we will return to in detail in our consideration of the concept of simulation in **Chapter 7**.

SOCIAL THEORIES OF MEDIA INTERACTIVITY

Manovich, in line with his approach to interfaces (**see Chapter 4**), offers a technically informed analysis of different types of media interactivity. This provides a useful introduction and overview to the technical basis of interactivity across a range of different media: new and so-called old (a distinction we question in the conclusion to this book). But interactivity might also be considered in sociological terms. This is the approach of Spiro Kiousis in his article 'Interactivity: A Concept Explication' (2002). Kiousis opens this paper with a word of caution, noting that 'many scholars have highlighted the confusion embedded in theoretical discussions surrounding the concept of interactivity and the subsequent problems it raises in research' (Kiousis 2002: 356). His response is to ask 'among other things, whether interactivity is a characteristic of the context in which messages are exchanged; is it strictly dependent upon the technology used in communication interactions; or is it a perception in the users' minds? (Kiousis 2002). This psycho-sociological approach to the question of interactivity is potentially at odds with more technically focused definitions such as those forwarded by Manovich. For Kiousis suggests, by contrast, that the experience of interactivity may not simply be the product of technical systems, but may also relate to the user's *sense* of this interaction and to the desired effects he/she wishes to produce from his/her machines.

The difficulty Kiousis raises is whether interactivity is something technological or human, or perhaps both (see Beer 2007). Kiousis observes that in the majority of new media literature to date interactivity is 'anchored in its ability to facilitate interactions similar to interpersonal communication' (Kiousis 2002: 356). This suggests a tendency to anthropomorphize new media technologies so that they are viewed as mirroring the world of human to human interaction. This is not something we can consider in detail in the present chapter, but it raises, in turn, another import-ant question: how might interactivity in technological systems be measured or compared to that in interpersonal communications, for the 'standard for what makes one medium more interactive than another is quite ambiguous' (Kiousis 2002). Manovich bypasses this difficulty by focusing on the structures of technical systems and measuring their interactivity in terms of a variable scale, which ranges from 'closed' to 'open' (although it is never altogether clear exactly how this scale is graded). In Manovich's approach, the question of human agency does not feature, as interactivity is seen to be a product of different media systems. But differentiating between different types of interactivity becomes more complex if, following Kiousis, human agency is introduced as a variable – that is, if systems are seen to vary in terms of interactivity depending upon who is engaging with them and in what context. For if this is the case, interactivity is less a product of system hardware than a consequence of social or psychological factors that shape the use and underlying design of media interfaces.

For Kiousis, this means that there are two sides to the study of interactivity: first, a scale of interactivity informed by an analysis of how a given technical system oper-ates, where 'interactivity levels only fluctuate by altering technological properties' (Kiousis 2002: 357), and second, a scale informed by the assertion that 'interactivity levels rise and fall within a medium dependent upon people's perceptions' (Kiousis 2002). The former of these tends to be the focus of computer-science literature which, in similar vein to the work of Manovich, centres on the technical design, structure and operation of media and their interfaces. It also lies at the heart of post-human approaches to technology and culture that see the human and the social as outcomes of technological development (see **Chapter 3** and **Chapter** 7). The latter, in contrast, lies at the centre of more humanistic approaches to technology that place a social actor at the centre of analysis, and see technological innovation as the product of human invention and creativity. A prime example of such an approach is Manuel Castells' *Internet Galaxy* (see Gane 2005b). Kiousis, meanwhile, signals the possibility of bringing these two sides into dialogue by outlining different qualitative scales along which interactivity might be conceived and schematized, although exactly how this is to happen remains far from clear.

Kiousis' analysis is to some extent broadened by Tanjev Schultz in his paper 'Mass Media and the Concept of Interactivity'. This paper opens by warning that 'one needs to be very careful when applying the term *interactive*' for this term too often lacks 'precise explication' (Schultz 2000: 209). Schultz responds by reassessing the continuities and disjunctures between the types of interactivity that are characteristic of media prior to and post the Internet age. Schultz argues that new media interactivity is different to the kinds of two-way or reactive communication that mass media traditionally relied upon to encourage audience involvement (such as letters or polls). New media interactivity is, for a start, instantaneous, and tends to work in 'real-time'. It also, in theory, offers the promise of being more democratic: 'the formal characteristics of fully *interactive* communication usually imply more equality of the participants and a greater symmetry of communicative power than one-way communication' (Schultz 2000: 210). The important term in this sentence, which is all but absent in the analyses of Manovich and McLuhan, is *power*. Importantly, Schultz asks whether the distribution of power between users and within technical systems has implications for interactivity and communication (something we will return to in our analysis of Kitter's protected mode in **Chapter 7**). His answer is that in many cases the 'use of ... new technologies is far from interactive' (Schultz 2000), for it is possible for so-called interactive new media to be deployed in ways that inhibit user interactivity. This position separates Schultz from Manovich, for it is based on a communicative model of interactivity in which it is not the interactivity of new media technologies themselves that counts per se, but rather the forms of interaction they facilitate or perhaps hinder between users. This returns us to the approach of social network analysts such as Barry Wellman that we described in **Chapter 2**, for the focus here is on how media are organized to structure communications in specific ways rather than the interactions between users and new media devices in themselves.

This connection of power and new media technology is explored from a different angle by Andrew Barry in his book *Political Machines* (2001: 128–52). In this work, Barry analyses interactivity as a concept that is tied to a contemporary political ideal of active citizenship. His argument is twofold. First, he notes that 'the individual citizen is increasingly expected, and increasingly expects, to make his or her own judgements about scientific and technological matters' (Barry 2001: 127–8). Second, this shift toward the individualization of political and perhaps ethical responsibility is not necessarily accompanied by a movement toward the heightened freedom or agency of individuals (something we touch upon in our analysis of the individualization of archives in **Chapter 5**). Instead, it is accompanied by the increased agentic powers of objects or technologies, and new modes of governance that place political rights and responsibilities firmly on the shoulders of individuals. Barry explains: 'Today, interactivity has come to be the dominant model of how objects can be used to produce subjects. In an interactive model, subjects are not disciplined, they are *allowed*' (2001:129). He demonstrates this argument by taking the modern science museum as an example. While this might come as something of a surprise to the reader, a strong rationale underpins this exercise: 'first ... science museums have played a significant part in the history of interactive technique and the idea of interactivity', and 'second, and more importantly, an analysis of the museum of science is suggestive of the way in which interactivity is actually much more than a particular possibility inherent in the development of media' (Barry 2001). This second point is central to Barry's argument. For in response to objections that new media are not truly interactive but 'create the illusion of choice' from 'a predetermined set of options' (Barry 2001:140) (thereby giving rise to new forms of 'interpassivity'), Barry argues that interactivity is not something confined simply to the technical operation of machines. Rather, it is to be thought of against the backdrop of a changing political landscape in which we are encouraged to become active citizens. He explains that

> [f]or advanced liberalism, the task of the public authorities is not to direct or provide for the citizen but to establish the conditions within which the citizen could become an active and responsible agent in his or her own government. Seen in this context, interactive devices had a function, for they might foster agency, experimentation and enterprise, thus enhancing the self-governing capacities of the citizen. (2001:135)

What is at stake here, for Barry, is the emergence of a political culture that governs not through discipline but rather through interactivity. Others have charted such a shift in terms of a movement from a regime of power based on coercion to one based on seduction (see for example Bauman 1998). But Barry's focus is slightly different as he examines the political injunctions that underpin the formation of contemporary citizenship and the technological devices through which they are subsequently embodied. This new 'interactive' universe is encapsulated by the following shift in emphasis: from 'Learn!' and 'You must!' to 'Discover!' and 'You may!' (Barry 2001: 150).

Barry is not alone in viewing museums as interactive environments that might be used to raise deeper questions about the political dynamics of the new media age. Anna Reading, in a paper entitled 'Digital Interactivity in Public Memory Institutions', analyses the use of new media devices in Holocaust museums. In particular, she looks at the ways in which such devices shape or perhaps even alter our notion of history and/or memory – something that is also addressed in **Chapter 5** in our consideration of digital archives. Reading's basic argument is that

> [t]he role of digital interactive technologies, and their use by museums and their visitors raise important issues about the form and effectiveness of 'interactivity' and about the tensions between visitor agency versus shared memorial experience. (2003: 71)

She adds that, perhaps surprisingly, there has been

> little complex exploration of how digital multimedia interactivity in relation to museums of history, and particularly museums of the Holocaust, may raise different questions from interactivity in a museum of science and technology, and how this may have particular implications for media-related learning and socially inherited memory. (2003: 73)

Reading argues that it is through detailed analysis of institutional settings, such as museums, and of how interactive media are deployed within such settings, that we can understand the complex ways in which new technologies mediate the public understanding of historical events such as the Holocaust. What is important for Reading, in some ways as for Barry, is for us to think about the institutional deployment of interactive media, and in so doing consider how such media not only reproduce memories but potentially change the basis of how and thus *what* we may know. This suggests that interactivity is not simply a technical interaction between a device and a user in a museum space, but rather a process through which 'public memories', knowledge and culture are mediated more generally. This complex set of connections cannot be explored in any detail here; but it can be observed, in light of the above, that the concept of interactivity has an underlying political charge.

INTERACTIVITY AND USER-GENERATED CONTENT

In the above sections we considered understandings of interactivity based upon the technical properties of media systems (Manovich), the social contexts and experiences that frame the uses of such systems (Kiousis), and the power dynamics that structure communication and information access through new media technologies (Schultz, Barry, Reading). Through analysis of these positions it is possible to outline at least four types of approach to the concept of interactivity. The first is a technically informed or structural vision of interactivity in which interactive potentials are built into the hardware and software of different media systems. The second defines interactivity in terms of human agency, and sees human involvement and freedom of design or use as the defining variables. Third, interactivity can be used as a concept to describe communication between users which is mediated by new media, and which gives rise to new possibilities for interpersonal communication. And finally, interactivity can be seen as a political concept that is tied to broader changes in governmentality and citizenship.

A key contemporary development that is of particular interest to the latter of these approaches is the emergence of 'Web 2.0' technologies that enable the production and mass circulation of *user-generated content* (see our analysis of the archive in **Chapter 5**). This development is accompanied by a new form of interactive culture in which users act at the same time as producers, for they participate in the construction of online spaces while at the same time consuming the content generated by others (see Beer and Burrows 2007; Ritzer 2007). For this reason among others, Web 2.0 demands that we think in new ways about the concept of interactivity. The following questions are particularly pressing: how is interactivity today structured by the software or underlying hardware of media machines (something we will consider in **Chapter 7**)? In what ways are Web 2.0 applications 'interactive', and how do they compare with older web applications (referred to in this rhetoric as Web 1.0) and with previous user-controlled media forms such as fanzines or newsletters? How do technologies that promote user-generated content shape human interactions, access to information, and our sense of collective and individual memory? What kinds of information do new forms of online interactivity create, what happens to this information, how is it used and with what consequences? The concept of interactivity might prove useful for examining the dominant rhetoric and understandings of new online cultures of user-generated content, which tend to tell us of the power of new media to liberate and democratize online space (see the discussion of Web 2.0's 'rhetoric of democratisation' in Beer and Burrows 2007). If used in this way, this concept could act as a critical tool for analysis of new media

Case Study: Last.fm

A pressing question to be encountered in the study of interactivity is how we are to understand the interactions between increasingly predictive or 'intelligent' media technologies and their users. For example, websites are emerging that attempt to predict the kind of music we might want to listen to based upon the types of music we or 'people like us' tend to like — whether this be the rock of Van Halen or the pop of Kylie Minogue. One such website is www.last.fm. Visitors to this site can select a favourite performer or group and this opens a 'radio station' that plays music that is similar to that of the selected performer. This, presumably, is organized by the tags that other users have attached to particular songs, and by the taste preferences of others that are marked out as being similar to our own. The radio station works by playing songs that are similar to those of the chosen artist, and the listener is invited to respond positively or negatively to the song that is selected. After this process has run a number of times and Last.fm has built up a profile of the type of songs that have been

– analysis grounded in technical systems (to gain an understanding of how these harvest and use information about us), in points of interaction between humans and machines (what might be called interfaces, see **Chapter 4**), and in the ways technologies are 'remediated' into everyday life.

This can be demonstrated through brief consideration of a mundane example: the website of the global online retailer Amazon. For some time, Amazon has devoted space on its website for users to rate a book or product and to post a review about that item. These reviews may, in turn, be rated by visitors to the page, and above each review is a line that states how many people have found that review to be of use in making their purchasing decision. This 'interactive' space is coupled with more formal information about a given product, along with a list of what other customers are browsing, and an archive of what people who bought a particular product also purchased. This is an example of a fairly routine online environment, but even so it is tricky to conceptualize, for in Manovich's terms both open (the reviewing spaces) and closed (the rating functions) forms of interactivity are situated alongside one another in a common space. To complicate this further, Amazon has also recently added a 'customer discussions' section which encourages the visitor to 'Ask questions, Share opinions, Gain insight'. This section is located below the customer reviews, and is presumably intended to cultivate a greater level of 'interaction' between visitors to the page by encouraging them to exchange views about different products. This production and circulation of user-generated content is, in many ways, close to the vision of interactivity considered above by Schultz, which

liked, a new 'radio station' is created that is specific to the user's predicted tastes. This station is just for that individual user and is honed as the profile continues to develop. Over time the user's profile becomes richer as more information is gathered, and as a result the radio station is able, at least in theory, to fine-tune itself to our individual tastes. This information enables a level of anticipation on the part of the technology, and is underpinned by a range of software algorithms that enable the required connections to be made. This

presents us, in turn, with the challenge of rethinking the concept of interactivity against the backdrop of new media technologies that are increasingly powerful in their ability to predict and perhaps even shape our tastes and preferences as users. This question of technology and human agency is something we return to in *Chapter 7*.

ties interactivity to communication and to the user's sense of interaction. However, the interactive structures of commercial websites such as Amazon are designed to market and ultimately sell products. With this in mind, commercial websites are often programmed to gather information about their visitors – the pages or objects they have viewed, what they have purchased or added to their wish-lists, and so on. This 'interaction' creates content that we can see on the website, but also produces a massive dataset that is less visible to the visitor. This dataset, which is made up of traces that are left behind in the course of such interaction, can then be 'mined' to produce fine-grained definitions of different consumer populations and their preferences. In sum, interactive media produce information about their users that is often of economic worth.

In light of this, it can be argued that interactivity is tied in multiple ways to the operation of the capitalist market, in which today information is a – if not *the* – primary commodity (see **Chapter 3**). This is one of the central ideas of Nigel Thrift's *Knowing Capitalism* (2005), which among other things addresses the meshing of software with the spaces and practices of everyday life. Thrift argues that in the West consumption 'has been boosted to such an extent that it has begun to produce new commodity forms bound up with new kinds of relations', and that these relations in turn are 'intimately bound up with the increasing mediatisation of everyday life' (Thrift 2005: 7). A key aspect of this process of mediatization is that, increasingly, as we consume through new media technologies we produce information about ourselves that in turn is of value to the capitalist market. Such processes are increasingly of interest to social scientists. For example, Joseph Turow's (2006) recent work, *Niche Envy*, illustrates how such transactional data might be used to discriminate between consumers by giving priority to those that they imagine to be most profitable. The connection of such data with geodemographic classification systems that use information to make predictions about our lives and neighbourhoods takes this a step further (Burrows and Gane 2006), for it enables the fine-grained mapping of different consumer groups in real space and increasingly real time. Interactivity viewed from this perspective is about us routinely giving up data as we interact with networked media that retain traces of our choices and preferences and in turn feed them back into our lives on the ground. Against this backdrop, it is important that new media interactivity is understood not simply as a technical phenomenon or as a source of user freedom, but as something that has an intimate and complex connection to the underlying dynamics of contemporary capitalist culture. Such a connection is hinted at in the work of Barry (see above), but detailed and sustained critical analysis is required that goes beyond the analysis of citizenship to address the positioning of the concept and ideal of interactivity within the discourses and dreams of the capitalist marketplace more generally.

CONCLUSION

We started this chapter by claiming that there was more to interactivity than might at first be thought, and in conclusion we are left with a vision of interactivity that is complex, and which is embedded in a range of debates concerning the classification of media as 'old' or 'new', the connection of technical and human agency, and the changing basis of life within 'fast' or 'knowing' forms of capitalism. Faced with such complexity, it is perhaps not surprising that interactivity is treated with some caution by the thinkers addressed in this chapter. What unites these thinkers, however, is a shared concern for rethinking this concept, even if in practice they develop quite different visions of interactivity. In the course of such rethinking, one thing is apparent: that interactivity cannot simply be used as a catch-all term to distinguish between an analogue and digital age, or between old and new media. Instead, as Manovich suggests, it is necessary to think of variable scales and types of interactivity, and to explore this concept through a historical understanding or genealogy of digital media. The reservations expressed by Manovich about the newness of 'new' media are well-placed. For rather than appealing to general classifications of media old and new, perhaps more useful is analysis that is sensitive both to historical context and to the remediation of contemporary life, and which refuses to abstract ideas or ideals of interactivity from their workings in concrete settings. It is here that an analysis of user-generated content as a concrete instance of contemporary interactivity might prove useful, particularly if it allows us to generate a more developed version of this concept while at the same time putting it to work to gain an understanding of the emergent world of Web 2.0.

At a more general level, one thing that is striking is the potential connectivity of the concepts considered thus far in this book. Interactivity in particular is situated within a network of other concepts. If it is considered, for example, in terms of communication (as in the work of Kiousis), we might ask of the networks (**Chapter 2**) or archival technologies (**Chapter 5**) that underpin interactive media and to which we may connect. The concept of interactivity also returns us to the analysis of information in **Chapter 3**, and to the value of (user-generated) data to the capitalist marketplace. More obviously, the very notion of interactivity presupposes the idea of an interface (**Chapter 4**) that enables communication between humans and machines, or perhaps simply between machines, with different interfaces providing different experiences of interactivity. This suggests that no single or lone-standing concept will suffice for the analysis of new media – something we return to in the conclusion of this book (see **Chapter 8**), where we argue for the development of a toolbox of concepts that can be used to explore the complex social and cultural dynamics of the digital age. With this in mind, we turn in the following chapter to the concept of *simulation*.

Chapter Summary

- Interactivity is a broad concept that can be applied to the analysis of human–human, human–machine and machine–machine connectivity.

- Interactivity can be thought of in social, psychological and technical terms.

- New media are not more or less interactive than analogue media forms, but are interactive in a different way.

- Interactivity often produces information that is of value to the capitalist market.

- There are important connections between the user-generated world of Web 2.0 and new forms of 'knowing capitalism' (Thrift).

7 SIMULATION

Simulation is no longer that of a territory, a referential being, or a substance. It is the generation by models of a real without origin or reality: a hyperreal.

Baudrillard (1994: 1)

Throughout the late 1980s and early 1990s, simulation was something of a buzzword in cultural and media studies. This was largely due to the impact of the writings of Jean Baudrillard, many of which first became available to an English-speaking audience around this time. Other cultural theorists, most notably Guy Debord, Umberto Eco and Paul Virilio (see Cubitt 2001), have advanced theories of simulation, but for the purposes of the present book, Baudrillard is taken to be *the* key theorist of this concept. In a number of dazzling texts, in particular *Symbolic Exchange and Death* (1993a) and *Simulations and Simulacra* (1994) (first published in French in 1976 and 1981 respectively), Baudrillard advances a theory of Western culture that is characterized by simulation and *hyperreality* (a term we will address below). Baudrillard's writings on simulation have been enormously influential, and have inspired creative new approaches to the analysis of a range of cultural phenomena and processes, most notably consumption and globalization (Perry 1998) and war (Der Derian 2001). Today, however, Baudrillard's work on simulation is less prominent in media theory, cultural studies and sociology. This is perhaps because simulated media environments are now so ubiquitous that they are taken for granted rather than placed under critical scrutiny. There has also been a subtle shift in the focus of contemporary media theory, which now rarely looks at simulation simply in itself, but rather at deeper connections between simulation and its material underpinnings. Such work raises new and important questions about the interplay of hardware and software, body and consciousness, physical and virtual space, and what might be called the *posthuman*. Two key thinkers in raising such questions are Friedrich Kittler and Katherine N. Hayles. This chapter will open by outlining the main features of Baudrillard's writings on simulation before moving, in turn, to a detailed analysis of the respective positions of Kittler and Hayles. In so doing, the chapter will revisit and extend a number of key themes and questions that have be addressed in previous chapters, including the connections between virtuality and embodiment (**Chapter 3**), and user interactivity and system control (**Chapter 6**).

ORDERS OF SIMULACRA

As stated above, the most striking and original theorization of simulation to date is to be found in the work of Jean Baudrillard. The main text of interest here is 'The Order of Simulacra', which forms the second chapter of his wide-ranging and notoriously difficult book *Symbolic Exchange and Death*. This chapter is remarkable as it charts the development and trajectory of Western culture in terms of a movement through three orders of simulacra or modes of appearance. While this might seem, on first reading, to be a rather odd way of understanding Western history, in fact its underlying intention is quite straightforward: to trace the shift from producer to consumer society, and to do so in terms of thinking about the connections between objects, signs and technologies. Baudrillard begins this exercise with the Renaissance, which, he argues, is characterized by cultural production that works to 'counterfeit' nature. This world of the counterfeit is tied to an economy of signs that emerges with the decline of the feudal order – signs that mark out new hierarchies of social status and social standing within the early modern period. Baudrillard hence declares that 'simulacra do not consist only of the play of signs, they involve social relations and a social power' (1993a: 52).

This economy of signs (which in the Renaissance is still restricted, even though it is freer than in feudal society) and its associated social or status order changes dramatically with the shift from the Renaissance to industrial society. For now, the emphasis is no longer on the copying or counterfeiting of nature but rather on the mass production of identical things that no longer have their roots in nature. Baudrillard illustrates this shift by drawing a distinction between the automaton and the robot. In a key passage, he explains that

> [a] world separates these two artificial beings. One is the theatrical, mechanical and clockwork counterfeit of man where the technique is to submit everything to *analogy* and to the simulacrum-effect. The other is dominated by a technical principle where the machine has the upper hand, and where, with the machine, *equivalence* is established. The automaton plays the man of the court, the socialite, it takes part in the drama of pre-Revolutionary France. As for the robot, as its name implies, it works; end of the theatre, beginning of human mechanics. The automaton is the *analogon* of man and remains responsive to him ... The machine is the *equivalent* of man, appropriating him to itself as an equal in the unity of a functional process. This sums up the difference between first- and second-order simulacra. (Baudrillard 1993a: 53)

In the industrial age, or the second order of simulacra, it is no longer the reproduction of nature but rather the mass production or 'indefinite reproducibility' of things that counts. This marks the birth of a culture in which the *series* – the 'possibility of two or *n* identical objects' (Baudrillard 1993a: 55) – rather than the reproduction of an 'original' form (which need no longer exist) takes primary significance. Baudrillard's analysis is here comparable to that of Walter Benjamin, whose study of the work of art in the age of mass production considers the extent to which objects are stripped of their aura once they become technically reproducible. Baudrillard states that Benjamin was 'the first (with McLuhan after him) to grasp technology as a medium rather than as a 'productive force' (at which points the Marxian analysis retreats), as the form and principle of an entirely new generation of meaning' (Baudrillard 1993a: 56). The key point, for Baudrillard, is that technology – including that of the factory – is always a form of media, the power of which lies in its ability not just to produce but to *reproduce* signs and objects. Indeed, in a provocative move Baudrillard declares: 'Benjamin and McLuhan saw more clearly than Marx, they saw that the real message, *the real ultimatum, lay in reproduction itself.* Production itself has no meaning: its social finality is lost in the series. Simulacra prevail over history' (1993a).

This shift away from a focus on production to reproduction and consumption is made clear by the introduction of a third order of simulacra, which in turn separates Baudrillard from Benjamin: the order of *simulation*. In Baudrillard's view, the age of industrial production is short-lived for 'as soon as dead labour gains the upper hand over living labour ... serial production gives way to generation through models' (Baudrillard 1993a). At this point, a third order of simulation is said to emerge: 'there is no more counterfeiting of an original, as there was in the first order, and no more pure series as there were in the second; there are only models from which all forms proceed according to modulated differences. Only affiliation to the model has any meaning ...' (Baudrillard 1993a). For Baudrillard, this culture of simulation has three key and interrelated features. The first is that computer modelling can be used to design and 'crash-test' objects or ideas by running them through imaginary scenarios that predict and perhaps shape events before they take place. The second is that reality gives way to hyperreality – that which is more real than the real. Baudrillard talks, for example, of the 'hyperrealism of simulation', and suggests that technologies, in particular digital media, increasingly shape our capacity to know the world (including key events such as the Gulf War, see Baudrillard 2004), and as a consequence blur the boundaries between what is 'real' and what is virtual or 'appearance'. In these terms, reality is not understood to be a universal phenomenon, as is generally presumed, but rather is treated as a historically specific construct – one that is tied for the most part to the class antagonisms and social structures of industrial society (the world of second-order simulacra, see Baudrillard 1983; Gane 2004: 4–8). Finally, the order of simulation is founded on a world of code which, for Baudrillard, takes us beyond physical reality as it had previously been known. This world of code includes the surface codes of local or global signifiers, brands or logos (see Klein 2000) that characterize *consumer* society, as well as the deeper binary codes that both underpin and are produced by computational machines. Baudrillard also sees a shift toward binary values at all levels of culture, and declares that 'digitality is among us. It haunts all the messages and signs of our society, and we can clearly locate its most concrete form in the test, the question/answer, the stimulus/response' (Baudrillard 1993a: 62). For Baudrillard, not only can culture today be represented in binary code (as argued by Manovich, see **Chapter 4**), but increasingly presents itself as a series of binary alternatives: a yes or a no, a 0 or a 1. Culture thus becomes an informational form – an idea that is not far removed from the information science of Shannon and Weaver outlined at the outset of **Chapter 3**. Baudrillard, meanwhile, addresses this development by drawing out the key distinctions between mass production (order 2) and simulation (order 3). In sum, he argues that the industrial age is characterized by

> [s]imulacra that are productive, productivist, founded on energy, force, its materialization by the machine and in the whole system of production – a Promethean aim of a continuous globalization and expansion, of an indefinite liberation of energy. (Baudrillard 1994: 121)

By contrast, contemporary consumer society proceeds according to a different set of principles: 'information, the model, the cybernetic game – total operationality, hyperreality, the aim of total control' (Baudrillard 1994).

SOFTWARE/HARDWARE

Baudrillard's work on simulation proved to be enormously popular throughout the 1980s and 1990s, and inspired a wide range of work on simulated and hyperreal cultures. Nick Perry (1998), for example, draws on Baudrillard's theory of hyperreality to explore global cultures in which it is no longer possible to distinguish clearly between reality and representation, and which instead produce endless copies of cultural forms that are fundamentally the same (a process that has been addressed by George Ritzer 2003 in his theory of 'grobalization'). James Der Derian (2001), meanwhile, has developed Baudrillard's (2004) remarks on simulation into an analysis of contemporary warfare that explores the fading boundaries between violence and entertainment. For Der Derian (2001: xi), contemporary culture is underpinned by the emergence of a 'military-industrial-media-entertainment network' in which 'made-for-TV wars and Hollywood war movies blur, military war games and computer games blend' and 'mock disasters and real accidents collide', in the process of which new configurations of 'virtual power' are said to emerge. The most striking examples of such power are to be found in current forms of 'virtual' and 'virtuous' war which, for Der Derian, confuse and pixilate 'war and game on the same screen' (2001: xvi), and beyond this join 'the human mimetic faculty for entertainment and gaming' with 'new cyborg programs for killing and warring' (2001: xx).

However, while Baudrillard's work has been applied to the study of emergent cultures of simulation, it has also been called into question by a range of thinkers who have sought to reassert the material underpinnings of simulation. Baudrillard's claim that '[s]imulation is no longer that of a territory, a referential being, or a substance' (1994: 1) has proved to be particularly contentious. In **Chapter 4**, we considered attempts by urban sociologists such as William Mitchell to think of new media environments and interfaces in terms of their connections to lived, everyday spaces. This emphasis on space and place (against the so-called 'end of geography thesis' – see for example Negroponte 1996) implies that simulation very much has a territory and a substance. Along similar lines, new media theorists such as Friedrich Kittler and N. Katherine Hayles have called into question the idea of simulation by rethinking complex connections between hardware and software, and virtuality and the body. Kittler's work, which we have already encountered in **Chapter 3**, draws digital technology into question by returning to a key theme of cybernetic theory and information science: *control*. Kittler digs beneath the surface of so-called virtual culture to draw into question the deeper structures of power and control that it often conceals. This places Kittler in direct opposition to critical theorists such as Jürgen Habermas (1984), who in his epic *Theory of Communicative Action* argues for a separation of communicative and instrumental reason, or communication and *power*. For Kittler, such a separation is not possible, especially in an age in which power structures are embedded within the hardware of media technologies, and which elude the control of the user while at the same time structuring communication from within. Kittler addresses this development by analysing the material bases of computation and communication that underpin the emergence and operation of simulated environments. Two chapters of his book *Draculas Vermächtnis* [Dracula's Legacy] (1993) are central to this approach: 'There is No Software' (1997:147–55) and 'Protected Mode' (1997:156–68). We will consider these briefly in turn.

The former of these pieces – 'There is No software' – is in many ways an extension of Kittler's reading of McLuhan (see **Chapter 3**), for it proposes that the medium or *hardware* of digital technology structures the content it processes and produces, not vice versa. McLuhan warned that this fundamental connection between the medium and its message could easily slip from view, not least because the content

of communication tends to blind us to the technologies or media that make communication itself possible: TV programmes (the content), for example, blind us to the
fact that we are watching TV (the medium). Kittler shares this worry, and responds
by extending the logic of McLuhan's argument to the study of digital technologies.
He starts out by observing that the recent explosion in commercial software conceals
an accompanying process of implosion at the level of hardware. First, media are
becoming physically smaller as the forms of past technologies are remediated into
the content of new media (see **Chapter 4**). For example, the phone, the fax, the
camera, the VCR can now all be contained within a palm-held personal computer.
Second, as stated by Baudrillard, such machines represent and process the content
of all communication in the form of binary code. This code is all but invisible to the
human eye, for it is designed to be processed by machines that, in turn, follow their
own, preprogrammed rules of operation. Kittler goes beyond Baudrillard by looking
at the rules or 'operation codes' that underpin such technologies, and thus virtual or
simulated environments more generally. Such codes can be burnt into the circuitries
of hardware itself, and lie concealed deep beneath the graphical user interfaces
(GUIs) that are common to most software packages. For Kittler, this means that for
the most part we remain unaware of the hardware operations and power structures
that underpin technologies of simulation. In a key passage he declares that

> [p]rogramming languages have eroded the monopoly of ordinary language and
> grown into a new hierarchy of their own. This postmodern Tower of Babel
> reaches from simple operation codes whose linguistic extension is still a hard-
> ware configuration, passing through an assembler whose extension is this very
> opcode, up to high-level programming languages whose extension is that very
> assembler. In consequence, far-reaching chains of self-similarities in the sense
> defined by fractal theory organize the software as well as the hardware of writing.
> What remains a problem is only recognizing these layers which, like modern
> technologies in general, have been explicitly contrived to evade perception. We
> simply do not know what our writing does. (1997: 148)

Software, and by extension simulation, does exist, but only as the effect of an underlying hardware, and this hardware, as Kittler observes, conceals itself through the
course of its own operation. Kittler speaks of a 'system of secrecy' in which each
physical layer of the machine, from the basic input-output system (BIOS) upward,
hides the one immediately beneath it. For example, the direct operating system
(DOS) of the personal computer hides the BIOS that enables this system to run, and
applications (such as Word) hide, in turn, the workings of DOS. The end result of this
upward spiral is the illusion that there is nothing other than software or simulation,
for the underlying hardware of the machine or system remains hidden from both
the user and the programs executed. This system of closure reaches its highest form,

first, with the emergence of GUIs, which, for Kittler 'hide a whole machine from its users' (1997: 151), and second, with the accompanying implementation of protection software, which prevents '"untrusted programs" or "untrusted users" from any access to the operating system's kernel and input/output channels' (1997).

Kittler explores the system codes that sit beneath software and which generate simulated or virtual environments in further detail in his writings on the 'protected mode'. In technical terms, the protected mode is a mode of operation that in contrast to earlier 'real mode' systems enables access to extended (32-bit) memory and with this the possibility of multitasking in a stable environment. Simply put, the protected mode refers to a series of built-in functions that are designed to 'protect' the operating system and machine from its users: 'it means that you can't just expect that everything in the computer is there for you to mess with. You can't just take over an interrupt. You can't just change the video settings. You can't just change the CPU's operating mode' (Delorie, nd.). While on the face of it the protected mode promises greater computing power, Kittler objects to its underlying authoritarianism, and to the ways it defines and controls the perimeters and possibilities of a given system. It might be objected that there are communities of hackers that seek to open out such systems through techniques of reverse engineering ('figuring out what software that you have no source code for does in a particular feature or function' (Perry and Oskov, nd.)), but for the most part, users engage with computers at the level of software, blissfully unaware of the programs and processes that run beneath it. Kittler here reminds us that the apparent 'user-friendliness' of commercial software and systems is achieved at a cost, for it is the product of a range of deep-seated power structures and 'one-way functions' that structure usage according to predefined 'priorities, prohibitions, privileges and handicaps' (Kittler 1997: 160). These structures are self-concealing for they are preprogrammed and are quite often burnt into the kernel or silicon of the system itself. This means that they become largely immune to user intervention or 'hacking', for they restrict what the user may alter or even see: 'one can no longer examine the operands of the operations' (Kittler 1997: 158). Software, as stated above, plays a vital role in maintaining this situation by hiding the underlying processes of the machine from immediate view, while at the same time giving the impression of openness. For Kittler, such openness is an illusion generated by the underlying technologies of simulation. He gives the example of programs or *daemons* that run behind applications, and which structure possible usage while remaining out of view: 'You never see them, and yet they're constantly doing something for you ...' (Kittler in Kittler and Virilio 2001: 102). Kittler's position is, in sum, that while computer-based technologies promise heightened interactivity, in fact they introduce and conceal processes of subjugation in the interplay between hardware and software. In this way, the preprogrammed machine is seen to take control of the user, not the reverse (as is generally assumed): 'the commands of the applications we use command *us*' (Ostrow 1997: ix).

This idea that technology possesses the power to shape and control human lives, along with our very ability to think critically about what 'technology' and the 'human' actually are, poses a number of urgent questions to conventional forms of media studies and sociology. Rather than focusing on the meanings users attach to objects or machines, and by extension the agency of such users, Kittler looks instead at the ways in which meanings are generated by an underlying technological framework (what might be called a post-hermeneutical approach), and at the ways, subsequently, that these technologies exercise control over their users (of which the 'protected mode' is one example). In so doing, he, like Baudrillard (see for example 1983), draws into question notions of 'human' agency and 'the social' – notions that mainstream theory for the most part treats as timeless forms that are resistant to technological intervention. The question Kittler's work begs is: in an age of 'intelligent' machines what does it mean to be *human* or *social?* This question is brought to the fore by Kittler's attempt to dispense with the discrete human actor or subject as an a priori fact or form. His approach refuses to read technology as something socially produced (the humanistic Marxist reading) or as something that is relevant insofar as it is subjectively meaningful (the Weberian line). Rather, it analyses the wide array of media technologies that make both *the social* and *meaning* possible.

This approach, which treats new media technology as an active agent of cultural change, is to some extent consistent with Baudrillard's theory of simulation, as outlined above. But Kittler takes things a step further by arguing that the idea of the 'human' is to be explained rather than presupposed, and that today such questioning should proceed from the analysis of new media technologies, in particular operating systems and silicon circuitries. Kittler employs precisely this methodology in his analysis of power: 'To begin with, one should attempt to abandon the usual practice of conceiving of power as a function of so-called society, and, conversely, attempt to construct sociology from the chip's architectures' (Kittler 1997: 162). The logic of Kittler's argument is clear: the increased and often invisible powers of technological systems to structure that space traditionally thought of as being 'human' are to be placed at the centre of critical analysis. Kittler goes beyond simply an argument for the recognition of object-agency – an argument expressed in quite different ways by thinkers such as Latour and Baudrillard – to declare that media technologies are more than just objects; they are active producers and *processors* of information. On this basis, Kittler argues that the internal logics and coded routines through which such technologies work, and through which simulated environments operate and are produced, are to be a – or perhaps even *the* – key focus of sociology and media theory. He declares that the way forward is for sociologists to think not just about 'people', or computers as such, but also 'programs' (Kittler in Kittler and Virilio 2001: 103). He gives similar advice to students of media and cultural studies: 'They should at least know some arithmetic, the integral function, the sine function – everything about signs and functions. They should know at least two software functions' (Kitler 1996: 741). Kittler's emphasis is on the crossing of analysis of the physical workings of the components of a given communication system with (especially in the case of digital media) the study of how these components function at the levels of mathematics and code. This, in turn, forms the basis of a new method for studying (intelligent) machines and the simulated environments they produce. He terms this approach *information materialism*.

Some might object to the strong technological determinism of Kittler's position. But even for those that find the lack of space for human agency in Kittler's work unpalatable, it is worth taking his work seriously, not least by using it as a resource for asking questions about the underlying dynamics of the new media age. For as decisions are increasingly made for us by media systems that we often have little choice but to use, it is no longer exactly clear what the term determinism in the charge 'technological determinism' might mean. For as machines 'learn' to design and communicate with other machines with little human input, the power of technologies to structure social life and shape our lived environments is becoming ever stronger. Perhaps one way forward is to consider the possibilities and dangers contained within this new situation, which for Kittler demands close historical study of machines, programs and codes. Kittler's argument, however, is that such analysis should place human subjects at the centre of its concerns, for such subjects are to be thought of instead in connection to objects, technologies and forms of information that increasingly have their own lives. This, in turn, demands the development of a sociology and/or media theory that draws into question the connections between humans and new media technologies, and in so doing opens up a field of study that might be termed *posthuman*.

EMBODIED VIRTUALITY

The key figure in exploring this new landscape of the posthuman is Katherine Hayles (see also **Chapter 3**). The basic idea in Hayles's work is that it is wrong to split mind from body or software from hardware, for both consciousness and information are always embodied in a physical medium of some kind. For Hayles, simulated environments are never 'purely' virtual for they are underpinned by a range of different material technologies. This places her in opposition to Baudrillard who rarely, if ever, looks at the media technologies that work to produce simulated or hyperreal cultural forms. Hayles sees in Baudrillard a tendency to abstract simulated environments from the technologies that make them possible. She declares: 'If simulation is becoming increasingly pervasive and important, however, *materiality* is as vibrant as ever, for the computational engines and artificial intelligences that produce simulations require sophisticated bases in the real world' (2002: 6). Moreover, Hayles accuses Baudrillard of being 'too conservative to keep up with the transformative power of information technologies' (2005a: 86), for his theory of simulation is very much framed by the digital media of the 1970s and 1980s, and because of this now starting to look a little dated.

Baudrillard, however, is only one target of Hayles's critique, which extends more broadly to 'posthuman' theories of information that separate out information from the bodily or computational media in which it is situated. There are, she says, four main features of this type of 'informational posthumanism'. First, it 'privileges informational pattern over material instantiation' (Hayles 1999: 2). Second, it downplays the role of consciousness in the formation of human identity. Third, it treats the body as 'the original prosthesis we all learn to manipulate, so that extending or replacing the body with other prostheses becomes a continuation of a process that began before we were born' (Hayles 1999: 3). And finally, the human is configured so that it can be 'seamlessly articulated with intelligent machines' (Hayles 1999). Taken together, this adds up to the following complaint: 'In the posthuman, there are no essential differences or absolute demarcations between bodily existence and computer simulation, cybernetic mechanism and biological

---

Case Study: Guitar Hero III – Legends of Rock

A useful place to start looking at the question of simulation is in video games, particularly as new forms of interface are emerging that enable users to perform bodily movements which are replicated on the screen and which become integral to the game itself. The Nintendo Wii console is a key example, for its wireless hand-held controller can be used to play a tennis shot or to bowl at some pins in a virtual alley. In such games, there is a constant flow of information between the body and the machine, and bodily movements become part of a simulation that plays out in real-time.

This is one instance of what Hayles calls 'embodied virtuality'. To pick a specific example of this type of embodiment we can look at the popular and well known game Guitar Hero III: Legends of Rock. This is a game that allows the user to play guitar in competition against rock legends like the heavy-metal guitarist Slash. Played through a console such as the Xbox or Playstation, the game has a guitar controller or *interface* that enables the user to 'play' guitar (or to play at playing guitar) to a number of well-known rock music tracks (see http://www.guitarherogame.

organism, robot teleology and human goals' (Hayles 1999). Hayles's response is to configure an alternative reading of the posthuman by contesting the separation of materiality from information, which for her lies at the heart of Baudrillard's theory of simulation, and cybernetic theory and information science more generally, from the work of Norbert Wiener and Claude Shannon onward (see **Chapter 3**). Her argument is that information can never do away with matter or the body, because to exist it must '*always* be instantiated in a medium' (Hayles 1999: 13). For this reason, she talks not of computer simulation or hyperreality, but rather of *embodied virtuality*, and of new forms of subjectivity that are born out of the interface between bodies and computer-based technologies. This approach gives rise to an alternative form of posthuman realism: 'my dream is a version of the posthuman that embraces the possibilities of information technologies without being seduced by fantasies of unlimited power and disembodied immortality' (Hayles 1999: 5).

This vision, in turn, frames Hayles's *Writing Machines* (2002), which considers literary works in light of the inscription technologies through which they are produced. This places Hayles on the same ground as, but also in opposition to Kittler. On the face of it, Hayles and Kittler share the same starting point: a critical reading of first-wave information theory and a concern for the underlying materialities of software simulations. Like Kittler, Hayles questions many of the liberal presuppositions that underpin early information theory and cybernetics, along with the assumption that information can be abstracted from all underlying material contexts, conditions

com/gh3/). Through a relationship with the guitar manufacturers Gibson and Kramer, guitar controllers are made to look like guitars, even if they are not played in the same way. The manufacturer suggests that this realism provides the user with a 'fully immersive concert experience', especially as it weds detailed venues, characters and sounds that together make this virtual environment more 'real'. This blurring of the real and the virtual lies at the heart of this game: the user plays on a controller that is designed to simulate a guitar, s/he creates sounds that reproduce those found in a live environment, and watches her/his own bodily movements as they are replicated on screen through competition with a virtual guitar legend. It is likely that this type of wireless controller will continue to develop given the huge popularity of Guitar Hero and Wii. If so, these games will provide a focal point for developing understandings of the interconnections between the real and the simulation, the material and the virtual, and the body and information.

and practices. But where she departs from Kittler is in her emphasis on the human *body*. For Hayles, the posthuman cannot be thought of outside of the bodily practices through which information is mediated:

> I view the present moment as a critical juncture when interventions might be made to keep disembodiment from being rewritten, once again, into prevailing concepts of subjectivity. I see the deconstruction of the liberal humanist subject as an opportunity to put back into the picture the flesh that continues to be erased in contemporary discussions about cybernetic subjects. (Hayles 2002)

Her aim, then, is not to show either that 'man' is a machine or that a machine can 'function like a man' (the obsession of early cybernetic theorists such as Norbert Wiener, see Hayles 1999: 7), but rather, on the one hand to demonstrate the limitations of liberal conceptions of the human that place 'man' in control (p. 288), and on the other to assert the continued existence of the human body by bringing into view the material practices and interfaces through which bodies and machines meet – for machines 'remain distinctively different from humans in their embodiments' (p. 284).

While Kittler is sympathetic to the former of these two aims (the shattering of the illusion of increased human control), he is hostile to the latter (the attempt to place embodiment at the centre of analysis). For whereas Hayles critiques the abstractness of information theory through an emphasis upon the materiality of the human body, Kittler's media materialism moves in a different direction: from information theory to an analysis of the physical components of the communication system: 'Let us forget humans, language and sense and instead turn to the details of the five elements and functions of Shannon' (Kittler 2002: 44). In this approach, there is no attempt to prioritize embodiment; first, because the boundaries between bodies and machines are no longer clear (if they ever were): 'The age of media ... renders indistinguishable what is human and what is machine ...' (Kittler 1999: 146). And second, even if the human body continues to exist, it is taken – together with the very idea of humanness – to be a construction or effect of technology rather than an agentic force in its own right. Once again:

> [w]hat remains of people is what media can store and communicate. What counts are not the messages or the content with which they equip so-called souls for the duration of a technological era, but rather (and in strict accordance with McLuhan) their circuits, the very schematism of perceptibility. (Kittler 1999: xl–xli)

In line with McLuhan, Kittler's primary interest is in technology and its power to introduce changes into (post)human life and culture, not vice versa. But at the same time, Kittler argues that McLuhan does not go far enough, for his definition of a medium as an extension of 'man' continues to place the human body at the centre of things: 'McLuhan, who was by trade a literary theorist, understood more about perception than about electronics, and for that reason attempted to think about technologies from the perspective of the body and not vice versa' (Kittler 2002: 21). It is on this point that Kittler departs from McLuhan and from all human-centred media theory (including media studies that centre on either the user or *audience*), including the work of Hayles, which, in spite of its emphasis on the ways bodies and machines construct each other, still tends to prioritize the material practices of the former over transformative powers of the latter.

THE POSTHUMAN

What emerges from the writings of Kittler and Hayles is effectively a dispute over the status of the body in an age of high technology, for on one hand Hayles insists on the continued embodiment of information and consciousness, while on the other Kittler refuses to give the body any kind of analytical or ontological priority in his analysis. This tension is part of a wider debate over what might be called the 'posthuman' – a debate which to some extent has eclipsed earlier exchanges over the cultural effects of simulation. Today, the term 'posthuman' circulates well beyond the realm of media theory, and is now commonplace in contemporary literary theory; science studies; political philosophy; the sociology of the body; cultural and film studies; and even art theory. Given the contemporary currency of this term, we will pause briefly to reflect on what it might mean.

The origin of the concept of the 'posthuman' is hard to trace, but – as Hayles suggests – it appears to come from cybernetic theories of the 1940s, and more specifically from the writings of Norbert Wiener (Pepperell 2003: 169). Interest in this concept, however, can also be traced to a more contemporary source: Donna Haraway's *Simians, Cyborgs, and Women: The Reinvention of Nature* (1991) (also discussed in **Chapter 3**). While Haraway does not use the term 'posthuman' explicitly in this work, she opens up debate around this concept by calling into question three key boundaries that have helped preserve the sanctity of 'the human' as a self-contained being: those between humans and animals, animal-humans (organisms) and machines, and the realms of the physical and non-physical (Haraway 1991: 152–3). For Haraway, such boundaries are no longer secure, if indeed they ever were, for they are now breached by an array of new hybrid creatures or *cyborgs*. These creatures, which are both organism *and* machine, are defined as follows:

> hybrid entities made of, first, ourselves and other organic creatures in our unchosen 'high-technological' guise as information systems, texts, and ergonomically controlled, labouring, desiring, and reproducing systems. The second essential

ingredient in cyborgs is machines in their guise, also, as communications systems,
texts, and self-acting, ergonomically designed apparatuses. (Haraway 1991: 1)

This figure of the cyborg proved enormously influential throughout the 1990s, not
least because it shifted debate about the *inhuman* (Lyotard 1993), or the negative
power of technology and time to constrain and inhabit human life, to analysis of
how intelligent machines and new technologies of genetic modification alter the
basis of life in both negative *and* positive ways.

This age of high technology, in which the human body is no longer tied to 'nature' but is (in theory if not always in practice) increasingly open to technological
design and modification, and in which the notion of the human is relentlessly called
into question, might be called *posthuman*. Pepperell, in his *Posthuman Condition*,
describes the posthuman as a time in which 'humans are no longer the most
important things in the universe', where 'all technological progress of human society
is geared towards the transformation of the human species as we know it', and
where 'complex machines are an emerging form of life' (2003: 177). In our view,
however, the posthuman is not about 'progress' as such, but rather the emergence a
new culture of transversalism in which the 'purity' of human nature gives way to the
possibility or threat (depending on your view) of new forms of creative evolution
that blur the boundaries between species, systems and machines. The posthuman is
a condition of uncertainty (Pepperell 2003: 167–8) in which the essence or nature
of things is far from clear. Halberstam and Livingstone capture the spirit of this
condition in the following declaration: 'the "post" of "posthuman" interests us not
really insofar as it posits some subsequent developmental state, but as it collapses
into *sub-, inter-, infra-, trans-, pre-, anti-*' (Halberstam and Livingstone 1995:
viii). A key – although not necessarily stable – point of orientation for analysis of
posthuman culture and society is the body (analysed as both a materiality and a text).
Halberstam and Livingstone treat the posthuman as a series of 'nodes where bodies,
bodies of discourse, and discourses of bodies intersect (1995: 2). This approach, in
similar fashion to the work of Hayles, attempts to disrupt cybernetic readings both
of the human body as an information system (see, for example, Haraway 1991),
and of information as a probabilistic, bodiless form (as declared in the early work
of Claude Shannon and Warren Weaver, see **Chapter 3**). Against such readings, the
critical posthumanism of thinkers such as Hayles reasserts the embodied nature of
information and perhaps even technology, regardless of whether bodies themselves
remain 'human'. Catherine Waldby describes this development as follows:

> The term 'posthuman' has come to designate a loosely related set of recent
> attempts to reconceptualise the relationship between the rapidly transforming
> field of technology and the conditions of human embodiment. These attempts

are, generally speaking, a response to the cybernetic turn and the vitalisation of information ... (2000: 43)

The concept of the posthuman has also entered wider political debate over the meaning and future of the human, and of nature more generally, in an age of rapid technological change. These debates currently range from cyborg citizenship and the possibility of forging a posthuman democracy to the politics of nature and the challenge of governing science, and even extend into highly charged exchanges over abortion and the point at which human life can be recognized as such (Fernández-Armesto 2004: 148–50). These debates are made ever more pressing by the following paradox:

> Over the last thirty or forty years, we have invested an enormous amount of thought, emotion, treasure, and blood in what we call human values, human rights, the defence of human dignity and of human life. Over the same period, quietly but devastatingly, science and philosophy have combined to undermine our traditional concept of humankind. (Fernández-Armesto 2004: 1)

It is in this paradox that the value of the concept of the posthuman really lies: in the possibility of contesting and *rethinking* what we call human values, human rights and human dignity, and in doing so against the backdrop of fast-developing bio-technologies that open the idea and the body of the human to reinvention and potential redesign.

Such issues have become particularly prominent in recent debates over genetics and even the future of liberal democracy. Francis Fukuyama – appointed by George Bush to the President's Bioethics Council in early 2002 – is perhaps the most outspoken commentator on these subjects. In his book *Our Posthuman Future*, he argues vociferously for state regulation of new biotechnologies that threaten to change the basis of human nature. The main difficulty faced by Fukuyama in making this argument is defining what is meant by this term. In the first instance, he defines human nature as a statistical entity: it 'is the sum of the behaviour and character-istics that are typical of the human species, arising from genetic rather than environ-mental factors' (Fukuyama 2002: 130). But he also prioritizes the uniqueness of human language (p. 140), consciousness and emotions (p. 169). This 'stable human essence', he claims, is crucial as it underpins the basis of liberal democracy, and most notably the American constitution:

> The political equality enshrined in the Declaration of Independence rests on the empirical fact of natural human equality. We vary greatly as individuals and by culture, but we share a common humanity that allows every human being to potentially communicate with and enter into a moral relationship with every other human being on the planet. (Fukuyama 2002: 9)

While it is far from clear that 'natural human equality' is indeed an 'empirical fact', Fukuyama's argument about the posthuman is straightforward: if contemporary biotechnology can change the basis of human nature then it threatens also to change that which gives 'stable continuity to our experience as a species' (Fukuyama 2002: 7), and upon which all political rights are built. He warns that while it might be assumed that the posthuman world (the world of altered human natures) might look like life today – 'free, equal, prosperous, caring, compassionate' (2002: 218) – it is likely to be worse than we expect, for the waning of the natural rights of liberal democracy may well be accompanied by new, extreme forms of hierarchy and competition, and 'full of social conflict as a result' (Fukuyama 2002).

This presentation of life today as 'free, equal, prosperous, caring, compassionate' idealizes the existing state or 'nature' of things, and in so doing glosses over the fierce inequalities of global capitalism. Hayles, however, in a paper entitled *Computing the Human*, challenges Fukuyama on different grounds, for she argues that his belief that 'humans are special because they have human nature' is not only tautological but is also based on a false separation of human nature from technology. By way of response, she seeks to 'disrupt' his position by claiming that 'it must also be "human nature" to use technology, since from the beginning of the species human beings have always used technology'. 'Moreover,' she adds, 'technology has co-evolved throughout millennia with human beings and helped in myriad profound and subtle ways to make human nature what it is' (Hayles 2005b: 144). For Hayles, then, there can be no easy separation between technology and the contested realm of 'the human'. This, in part, is because advanced computer-based technologies have become a – if not *the* – reference point for defining 'humans' and for measuring their capabilities. Hayles observes that today 'rather than the human being the measure of all things, as the Greeks thought, increasingly the computer is taken as the measure of all things, including humans' (1998). In computer science, influential figures such as Ray Kurzweil, Hans Moravec and Rodney Brooks have explored possibilities for the future convergence of humans and machines by downplaying the differences between these entities. Computers are also key reference points for more conservative thinkers such as Fukuyama, who concentrates 'on those aspects of behaviours that machines are least likely to share' (Hayles 2005b: 132), most notably emotions. What unites these positions is that the computational machine is taken as a benchmark for defining and understanding what is 'human'. What separates them is their approach to history, for while Brooks, Kurzweil and Moravec, along with a whole host of science-fiction writers, have used the future to question 'the human', Fukuyama, by contrast, anchors human nature in the past, specifically in a 'history of human evolution' (Hayles 2005: 147) that also allows for the presence of a human soul (Fukuyama 2002: 170). Hayles, by way of response, refuses to address the posthuman through either backward-looking conservatism or futurology, but calls instead for 'principled debate' about how to 'achieve the future we want' (Hayles 2005: 148). In so doing, she reveals her own political preferences: 'What it means to be human finally is not so much about intelligent machines as it is about how to create just societies in a transnational global world that may include in its purview both carbon and silicon citizens' (Hayles 2005).

CONCLUSION

The theories of simulation and hyperreality forwarded by Jean Baudrillard in the late 1970s, while still influential, have largely given way to analyses of the complex materialities and technical processes that make simulation possible, along with fierce debate over the status of the human body in the new media age. Friedrich Kittler, on one hand, emphasizes the role of hardware in structuring media-driven environments, while Katherine Hayles, on the other, reminds us of the computational engines that sit beneath software simulations and of the embodied nature of information. This is not to say that the cultural logic of simulation as described by Baudrillard has simply disappeared, but that simulation is to be explained through reference to the materialities that make it possible and which, in turn, it helps shape. This tension between hardware/software, real/virtual, body/consciousness lies at the very heart of recent debates about the posthuman. In spite of this shift toward analysis of the posthuman, however, Baudrillard's concept of simulation has, in several respects, yet to be exhausted. For if his orders of simulacra are read genealogically rather than in linear fashion – as they are in Hayles (2002) – then simulation is not to be taken as universalizable or as a totalizing end point to history (as suggested by Cubitt 2001) but as one cultural logic among many. To take such a position, we perhaps have to work against Baudrillard himself, who states of the orders of simulacra that 'Every order subsumes the previous order. Just as the order of the counterfeit was captured by the order of serial reproduction ... so the entire order of production is in the process of toppling into operational simulation' (1993a: 57). Against this statement, it is possible to insist instead that simulation is *one* powerful dimension of a global culture that continues to have many competing logics and principles (which are both analogue and digital). This, in turn, opens possible lines for the analysis of a globalizing world in which different orders of production and value are drawn increasingly into contact and potential conflict with one another. This concern is central to Baudrillard's early work, which emphasizes the power of symbolic exchange – primordial forms of gift exchange that lie outside of the logic of Western orders of value – to disrupt the precession of simulacra. In the early 1990s, Baudrillard also added a fourth (dis)order to the scene – the fractal or viral (Baudrillard 1993b) – and this complicates things further. For while Baudrillard's notion of hyperreality has been widely used and debated, few have attempted to rethink simulation against the backdrop of chaos or fractal theory, or in connection to symbolic or singular forms that lie outside of Western culture. It is along these lines, and in the light of recent analyses of thinkers such as Hayles and Kittler of the embodied and/or material basis of the virtual age, that new conceptual definitions and understandings of simulation might be forged.

Chapter Summary

- New media technologies produce simulations that blur the boundaries between the 'real' and the virtual.
- Virtual environments are never free-floating: they have technical and material underpinnings.
- Computational machines that produce simulations are governed by underlying rules that are often inaccessible their users (Kittler).
- The human body continues to be of key importance even in a world in which new media simulations are commonplace (Hayles).
- Interest in the concept of simulation has been augmented by a new concern for the posthuman.

8 CONCLUSION

This book has stressed the importance of reassessing concepts as part of an ongoing theoretical project that seeks to make sense of the new media age. Rather than talking of concepts in static terms we have tried to read them alongside and against one another, and to put them to work to show how they might inform, and in turn be informed by, analyses of new media technologies. Concepts are never fixed or definitive tools of thought, and are only meaningful or 'good' insofar as they may be applied to the study of specific research problems. As stated in **Chapter 1**, concepts are not static entities that are easy to study, but are rather 'thinking technologies' that are deeply contested and can take on different powers according to the tasks to which they are put. For this reason, the present book in no way pretends to offer a definitive account of all concepts required for the study of the new media age, for such a task is by its very nature impossible. Instead, our ambition has been a modest one: to analyse in detail six concepts that are useful for the study of new media, and which, beyond this, might have a broader analytical scope and application within social and cultural theory.

In the course of this work, we have called into question concepts that in many cases have entered into everyday parlance – for example network, information and interactivity – and which today are so ubiquitous that it is easy to take them for granted. The reason for this is twofold: first, concepts often take on a different meaning and significance when they enter popular usage (or cross disciplinary boundaries), and second, if concepts are left unattended they can soon slip into a state of disrepair. Even concepts that appear lively and at the cutting edge of thought can rapidly become what Ulrich Beck has termed 'zombie categories': 'empty terms' that are 'living dead categories, which blind the social sciences to the rapidly changing realities inside nation-state containers, and outside as well' (Beck 2002: 24). 'Archive' (see **Chapter 5**) is one example of how a concept can atrophy if it is not informed by, and at the same time used to address, the world of which it is a part. The challenge this presents is to rethink the conceptual vocabulary of our times in connection with a range of concrete social and cultural phenomena. We have attempted to do this in the present book, but, as stated above, by no means is the conceptual vocabulary we have developed here exhaustive. There are many other concepts, both old and new, that this book touches upon but which require more detailed analysis ('protocol' and 'posthuman' are two examples), and which in turn may open up new forms of theoretical and empirical work. The network of concepts that we have assembled seeks to provoke engagement across disciplinary boundaries, and to prompt readers to question the conceptual imagination of the disciplines within which they work. The book is an invitation to the reader to reflect on the conceptual vocabulary required for analysis of the new media age, and to think, more deeply, about what concepts are and the purposes they serve. This, no doubt, is an ongoing project. We might, for example, continue to think of concepts anew against the backdrop of Web 2.0 as described in our analysis of the archive in **Chapter 5** and interactivity in **Chapter 6**. In so doing, the media technology which is under study might well play a part, for we can imagine a toolbox of wiki-concepts built out of user participation and updated in real-time in response to situations or emergent trends that demand immediate critical attention. At this point, concepts for the analysis of new media will perhaps give way to *new media* concepts that are faster-moving and more flexible in form than those we possess at present.

A NETWORK OF CONCEPTS

For the moment, however, it is worth reflecting on how the six concepts considered in this book might be placed into contact with one another to form a set of tools for the analysis of new media. For rather than preserving concepts as separate entities, they can be assembled into a network of 'thinking technologies' that might inform future analytical and critical work – a possibility considered in the conclusion to **Chapter 6**. This is not to say that the concepts considered in this book are to be synthesized to produce a meta-conceptual form, but that they can be used together while at the same time performing different tasks of analysis. For instance, if we are interested in understanding how people connect online and make friends in social networking sites, we might use the concept of network in conjunction with interface and interactivity, or perhaps network with archive. If our focus is instead the under-lying power structures of new media culture, each of the six concepts addressed in this book might be of use – but perhaps most importantly network, information and simulation. What we hope to have generated throughout this book is thus not six individual concepts that are designed to stand alone, but rather a broader network of concepts that is of use for the analysis of the new media age. To this end it is necessary to think of these concepts together to understand what each can do and how they might work collaboratively. Let us begin with a simple illustration of what such a network might look like (see Figure 1).

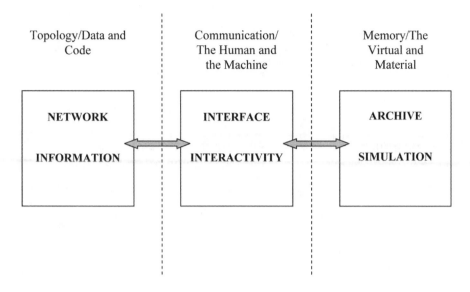

Topology/Data and Code	Communication/ The Human and the Machine	Memory/The Virtual and Material
NETWORK **INFORMATION**	**INTERFACE** **INTERACTIVITY**	**ARCHIVE** **SIMULATION**

Figure 1. A preliminary conceptual framework.

Figure 1 depicts a simplistic conceptual assemblage that moves between the structural and infrastructural concepts described at the beginning of the book (**network** and **information**), through concepts that deal with human-machine contact (**interface** and **interactivity**) to those that address the storage capacities of media and the lived environments they create (**archive** and **simulation**). As stated throughout this book, concepts are contested terms, the definitions and uses of which vary greatly – something that Figure 1 fails to represent. Indeed, the many thinkers addressed in this book start from different points in this framework and assign these concepts value to varying degrees. Castells, for example, prioritizes the concepts or metaphors of the *network* society and *information* age (**Chapters 2** and **3**), while Manovich focuses on the question of *interactivity* (**Chapter 6**) and Baudrillard on questions of *simulation* (**Chapter 7**). In each of these cases, these thinkers tend to work with a meta-concept that is tied to their different evaluative interests, and around which a broader conceptual framework is subsequently organized. But for us, given that this is a book of key concepts, there is no overriding meta-concept which should take immediate priority. Rather, our aim is to draw attention to the internal and external tensions between concepts, and to give an indication of how they might be put to work both on their own and in combination with each other. With this objective in mind, it is possible to think in a little more detail about how the six concepts considered might work together in the form of a non-hierarchical network or system. We attempt to clarify this in Figure 2.

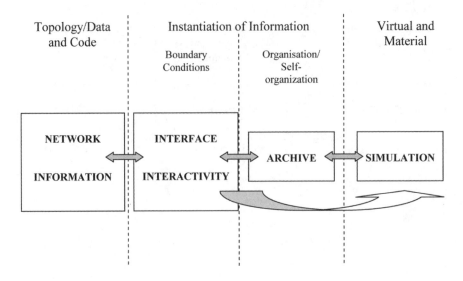

Figure 2. A preliminary conceptual framework, version 2.0.

Drawing upon the work of Hayles (1999), we can perhaps think of the concepts that lie at the heart of the above figure as mid-range concepts that deal directly with the ways in which information becomes materialized or embodied through various media. These are concepts that are useful for understanding the processes and practices through which information and networks come to be realized in our everyday lives – a point of interest that runs throughout this book. Concepts such as interface and interactivity, for example, are tools of thought that enable us to examine in close detail the connections between new media structures and user experiences. The concept of the archive, by contrast, might be used to address the ways through which information is organized or self-organized through interfaces that often give rise to new simulated environments, which in turn produce their own complex sets of (bodily and urban) materialities.

With this in mind, these concepts can be pushed further and developed into a more elaborate theoretical toolbox. In Table 1, we map some of the basic materialities associated with these concepts, along with some of the key debates or questions they help us explore. These materialities are important because new media are not objects out there; they are not autonomous devices separate from how we live. Instead, they are an integral part of our everyday lives and routines. New media are about people in places and organizations, and, by extension, about fast-moving forms of sociality and culture that both underpin and emerge from their use.

Table 1. A conceptual toolbox for the study of new media

Concept	Materialities	Key Debates
Network	• Technical infrastructures and topologies • Assemblages and connections • Inter-system operations	• De-centred or hierarchical? • Social or technical? • Individualized or collective?
Information	• Data • Coding • Flows and mobilities	• Probabilistic or material? • Non-discursive? • Commodified?
Interface	• Portal and access points • Cross-system exchange • Tactile media	• Virtual or material? • Human or technological? • Transversal?
Archive	• Storage of data and metadata • Formal and informal classifications or tagging • Multimedia/Web 2.0	• Post-discursive? • Self-centred or communal? • Technologized memory?
Interactivity	• Human-machine communication • Remediation • Subjectivity and citizenship	• Myth or reality? • Technical or human agency? • Connected to new forms of governance?
Simulation	• Hyperreality • Hardware and Software • Protected modes	• Real or hyperreal? • Human or posthuman? • Embodied?

SOME EMERGENT THEMES

Table 1 indicates how the concepts considered in this book might be deployed, both individually and collectively, to address specific aspects of the new media age. In forming this toolbox, it is worth considering at a more general level some of the common threads that run between these concepts, and thus between the chapters of this book. As stated at the outset, the concepts considered here are complex multiple forms that defy simple definition. For even where there are dominant meanings attached to concepts, there are also usually resistances and alternative readings to be found. This, in turn, has made the task of outlining a core body of new media concepts a difficult one, but it has also brought a number of important considerations to the fore. In particular there are four points we would like to reflect upon, albeit in brief.

First, *new media concepts often derive from disciplines that are concerned with the technical aspects of new media technologies*. We have not been able to explore the history of these concepts in any great detail, but nevertheless it is clear that in most cases they have a technical as well as social and cultural application. Information, network (particularly contemporary usages), interface and interactivity all fit into this category. These are terms that are used frequently by disciplines (such as computer science) that are concerned with the technical infrastructures and workings of new media systems. It is common for new media concepts to have been appropriated from these disciplines and recast to suit different social-science agendas. As part of this process, the meaning and uses of such concepts tend to shift dramatically, and bear little resemblance to their technical incarnations. This is something that we considered in our analysis of network at the outset of **Chapter 2**.

Second, *new media concepts can interface with one another*. Because new media concepts can be used to understand different aspects of new media (see above), we find that like the systems they are used to theorize they too have points of contact with one another. We can think of this as *the interfacing of concepts*. This means that rather than seeing concepts as competing terms that are fighting with one another for the same analytical territory, concepts can be used alongside each other to unlock a common analytical problem. This is illustrated by the two figures and table above. It means that a concept or body of concepts might be employed to address a specific evaluative interest or to analyse a particular aspect of a new media system. As stated previously, concepts allow for different types of analytical focus and can be used in conjunction with each other or separately depending on the research problem to be addressed. Beyond this, however, concepts might also act as intellectual interfaces that bring different theoretical systems into contact with each other, and thereby enable new cross-disciplinary work to be performed. This is something that is apparent in each of the previous chapters, which work across a broad range of theoretical material – from sociology, philosophy, media studies, cultural theory and computer science.

Third, *new media concepts provide a way of turning new media objects into social and cultural phenomena* while remaining sensitive to their underlying materialities. This is to say that new media concepts allow us to look beyond the technical working of a device by addressing it as a social and cultural phenomenon. This might be done in a variety of different ways, but the objective is usually to think of the technological as a part of the social and the cultural rather than as a world in its own right. For example, questions of power lie at the centre of conceptual analyses of networks, information, interactivity and simulation, and to address such questions it is necessary to move beyond technical description of media devices (which is nonetheless important) to understand their social and cultural dynamics. New media concepts can help us to make this connection. An example is 'archive', considered in **Chapter 5**. At face value, it would appear that the archive is a material technology rather than a conceptual form. But things are more complex than this, for it is a material (or increasingly virtual) technology that also has an underlying conceptual design. This in turn raises interesting questions about how concepts become materialized, and about whether their material operation might exceed or escape their intended usages. Aside from this, the conceptual basis of a technology might also tell us something about its wider social and cultural logic. The change in the archive from a public or state-centred form to a technology of self-display and popular memory, for example, might be used as a point of departure for thinking about new forms of sociality that are 'individualized' or 'liquid' in nature (see Bauman 2000, 2001b). Again, such analysis can only proceed by thinking beyond technology as something that is purely technical in form.

Finally, *conceptual analysis forces us to rethink the possibility of critical media theory in an age of accelerated social and cultural change*. A key difficulty to be confronted in writing about new media is that they are changing so rapidly that it is hard to keep up. This problem is not confined to the study of new media but applies to the analysis of accelerated social and cultural forms more generally (Gane 2006). This said, the problem is perhaps more acute in this particular field of study, for new media technologies play a key role in accelerating our everyday lives and are themselves accelerated forms. This poses a problem for conceptual work, for often ideas or technologies that we think are well established turn out to be to be ephemeral, leaving the history of media littered with technologies and concepts that have faded from view or which failed to quite make it in the first place. This presents us with a number of further challenges in this book. One challenge is that examples (including our boxed case studies) that can be used to illustrate the workings of concepts are intrinsically problematic, for they run the risk of being rapidly outdated. This begs a much broader theoretical question, one that cannot be dealt with within the confines of the present book: how is it possible to say anything remotely enduring in a world marked by accelerated forms of social and cultural change? (Gane 2006; Beer and Burrows 2007; Hardey and Burrows 2008) One preliminary answer might be to consider a formalized version of what the science-fiction writer William Gibson (2003) has called 'pattern recognition'. Pattern recognition is about spotting something when it is nascent and still a little out of the ordinary. This requires us to develop a sensitivity to social and cultural phenomena so that we may spot and respond to new movements in their early stages before they expand into the cultural mainstream. Like the central character Cayce in Gibson's novel, whose allergy to logos and branding causes a heightened sense of brand awareness, we could perhaps act as sociological 'cool-hunters' by getting an early sense of what is happening, and, in our case, attempting to forge appropriate conceptual tools of analysis.

This is important, for not only do theories and examples of digital phenomena date rapidly, so do the concepts we use to understand or analyse them. As stated at the outset of this chapter, concepts too can look old and dated in a very short space of time. A number of strategies might be employed by way of response. We might look to regenerate existing concepts in the light of the contemporary world, work toward a new conceptual vocabulary (in the manner of thinkers such as Baudrillard, Virilio and Deleuze), or maybe both. Older concepts (such as power or class) clearly still have much to offer, but often need to be worked alongside new concepts that emerge from, and are tied to, analysis of the new media age. If the aim is rather to develop a new conceptual vocabulary, then the question is of how, and from which theoretical or empirical resources, this is to be forged. It has been suggested, for example, that we may find new concepts in science-fiction literature (Burrows 1997), in design literature (Beer 2007), through engagements with new media industries (Lash 2007), or perhaps from the technical language of computer science (see **Chapters 2** and **3**). Again, the relative strengths of these resources (among others) for forging concepts for the study of new media will vary according to the particular problems and tasks to which these concepts are to be applied.

NEW MEDIA? A PARTING THOUGHT

One problem with prefixing media with the term 'new' is that it ties us into a constant struggle to keep up by attempting to study what appears to be new and emergent. This locks us into frenetic and unrelenting processes of following 'a little way behind change' (Thrift 2005: vi): trying to stay up to date or perhaps 'cool-hunt'. The tendency and problem of such an approach that it concerns itself with mobilities and disjunctures rather than with fixities and continuities. But there are alternatives. We could, for example, develop new media studies into a kind of social history, one that involves slower, more patient techniques of analysis that accept that new media studies is always already a historical exercise. Paradoxically, it might be the case that in an age of social and cultural speed-up the best response might not be to adhere to the logic of the capitalist market and to chase the 'new', but rather to take a step back and take stock of events. This approach, which in turn runs the risk of being left behind, has been advocated by Jean Baudrillard in his analysis of

September 11 (see Gane 2006). This is not something we can explore in any detail here, but it does prompt us to reconsider what counts today as being 'new' media. One response might be that 'new' media are no longer new – especially for users that have grown up in an age of digital technologies and mobile, networked devices. For this reason, among others, the idea of new media should be subjected to critical attention. This is something we have attempted to do throughout this book, but particularly in **Chapter 6** where we look at the use of concepts of interactivity to differentiate new from old media. We would like to conclude by returning to some of these key issues.

One of the main objections to the idea of new media is that many of the functions of such media are not all that new. Figures such as Manovich, Bolter and Grusin, and Graham hence talk of remediation rather than of 'new' technologies that have no clear social or technical history. In such an approach the digital or new media age is examined historically, and seen to be intimately connected with previous ages of media development (for examples, see Poster 1996; Kittler 1999; Hayles 1999). Manovich, for instance, observes that discrete representation, multimedia capability and random-access memory, which are commonly seen to be distinctive qualities of new media, are in fact to be rejected as principles for distinguishing between new and old media, for each is to be found, or at least prefigured, in early cinematic technologies. As we saw in **Chapter 6**, Manovich calls these three principles 'myths of the digital', for in spite of their appearance as contemporary phenomena they are not as new as they might seem. Moreover, he warns that the concept of the digital should itself be treated with caution, for it acts 'as an umbrella for three unrelated concepts – analog-to-digital conversion (digitization), a common representational code, and numerical representation' (2001: 52). Hence, when we use the term 'digital' we must be clear what we mean. Manovich's answer is to break down and examine the digital in terms of its constituent parts. This enables him to assert the historical continuity between 'new' and 'old' media, while at the same time drawing a line of demarcation between the two. This line is made possible because it is only in the computerization of media that these principles really come to the fore, or to use Manovich's own words, 'increasingly manifest themselves' (Manovich 2001: 27). In view of this, of the five principles of new media that are outlined by Manovich – numerical representation, modularity, automation, variability and transcoding – one is clearly to be given priority: that part of digitality that involves numerical representation, or to be more precise, the digital reduction of cultural objects to a standard numerical form. The processing of binary code is thus, for Manovich, *the* defining feature of new media technologies.

But there are other, less technical ways of thinking about this question of newness – some of which are addressed in a short introductory essay written by Roger

Silverstone for the first issue of what was then a new journal *New Media & Society*. Written in 1999, at a time when Internet-based technologies had started to achieve mass circulation, this essay asks: 'what's new about new media?' This basic yet difficult question, Silverstone suggests, is all too easily overshadowed by a fascination with the technical wizardry of new media, or what they can *do*. By way of response, Silverstone calls for a focus on the qualitative impact of such technologies rather than analysis directed toward their technical capacities. His position is as follows:

> The technologies that have emerged in recent years, principally but not exclusively digital technologies, are new. They do new things. They give us new powers. They create new consequences for us as human beings. They bend minds. They transform institutions. They liberate. They oppress. (Silverstone 1999: 10)

For Silverstone, to ask the 'question *"what is new about new media?"* is to ask a question about the relationship between continuity and change' (Silverstone 1999). He suggests that in order to apprehend the new it is necessary to rely upon established questions and approaches, at least in the first instance. This leads, in turn, to a call for a rigorous focus upon meaning, change, power and organization so that we are not 'blinded by excess', for 'new media pose new analytical challenges, but also reinforce old ones' (Silverstone 1999: 11). The question this begs is whether 'new' media do indeed bring something new, or whether many of the things we understand to be distinctive about them have been seen before. Silverstone appears to opt for the latter, declaring that 'The supposedly distinct characteristics of new media: digital convergence; many-to-many communication; interactivity; globalization; virtuality; are arguably, with the possible exception of the technical, not new at all' (Silverstone 1999). At this point, however, Silverstone appears to come full circle, and ends up close to the position of Manovich, for whom new media, ultimately, are seen to be new only on the basis of their technical capacities and prowess.

Today, now that we are more familiar with such media than at the time of Silverstone's essay, the problem has perhaps changed. For while new media are still as seductive as ever and often dazzle us with what they can do, they have become increasingly ubiquitous in advanced capitalist society. The danger of such ubiquity is that media become so woven into our everyday lives that we start to take them for granted. Marshall McLuhan anticipated exactly this situation back in the mid-1960s in *Understanding Media*, in which he warns that all media, once established with mass appeal, introduce a state of somnambulism in which it becomes increasingly difficult to detect – let alone question – their presence. The irony today is that this situation is exacerbated by the heightened dynamism or 'intelligence' of the technologies which surround us. Haraway sensed this tension back in the mid-1980s in her observation that 'Our machines are disturbingly lively, and we ourselves frighteningly inert' (1991: 152). There are good reasons, then, to suggest that the notion of 'new media' should be challenged in the same way that we have challenged the concepts that fit under its umbrella. This is something we have attempted to do throughout the course of this book, for 'new media' at best describes a changing field, and is often used too broadly to address contemporary developments with any accuracy or purpose. Moreover, as stated above, many of the central objects of new media studies – the networked computer, the mobile phones, the MP3 player – have been in mass circulation for over a decade now and are thus no longer new as such.

Perhaps, then, we should drop the term 'new media' and imagine instead a different umbrella term that would enable us to take a more nuanced and critical look at the interplay of emergent technologies, sociality and culture. This indeed is one option. But the term new media might not be the source of the problem. For if we were to remove it from our vocabulary we would still be faced with the difficulty of tracking and making sense of a world that is changing at an accelerated pace, and in which new technologies and social dynamics are emerging all the time – even if these do not break radically with the past. Our sense is that no umbrella term is flexible enough to deal adequately with this situation, which is why the world of new or digital media can only be addressed in detail through an array of conceptual devices, some of which are explored in this book. Such devices, it is hoped, enable us to maintain a lively, fresh and yet considered approach to the digital age as it continues to unfold. We would argue that this is especially important given the unprecedented speed at which both media and culture today move from being new to mundane.

QUESTIONS FOR ESSAYS AND CLASSROOM DISCUSSION

1 INTRODUCTION: CONCEPTS AND MEDIA

1. What is a concept?
2. What do Deleuze and Guattari mean by a 'pedagogy of the concept'?
3. Outline the key concepts needed for the study of new media.
4. What is it about new media that makes them 'new'?

2 NETWORK

1. What is a network?
2. Why might it be useful to study networks conceptually?
3. Why is it important to analyse the topologies and protocols of networks?
4. Critically assess Castells' idea of a 'network society'.
5. What are the main features of either a) social network analysis or b) actor network theory?

3 INFORMATION

1. Is the information science of Shannon and Weaver still useful today?
2. Is information a material property?
3. What is the difference between information and knowledge?
4. Is information a commodity?
5. What is meant by the term 'informatics'?

4 INTERFACE

1. 'The interface stands between the human and the machinic' (Poster). Discuss using a range of contemporary examples.
2. To what extent do interfaces make networks possible?
3. Critically assess Manovich's theory of cultural interfaces.
4. In what ways might new media interfaces give rise to new opportunities for power and surveillance?
5. Are interfaces conceptual as well as material forms?

5 ARCHIVE

1. Outline and assess the main arguments of Derrida's *Archive Fever*.
2. In what ways have new media technologies transformed the form and content of contemporary archives?
3. Do new media archives promote the individualization of culture?
4. Does the Internet alter our sense of collective memory?
5. How are new media archives governed?

6 INTERACTIVITY

1. What does Manovich mean by the 'myth of interactivity'?
2. Is interactivity primarily technical or social in basis?
3. Is new media interactivity tied to a new ideal of active citizenship?
4. How might interactive technologies aid the development of what Thrift calls 'knowing capitalism'?
5. What is Web 2.0?

7 SIMULATION

1. Outline and assess the key features of Baudrillard's theory of simulation.
2. Should we analyse simulation without considering the machines that make it possible?
3. What does Hayles mean by the term 'embodied virtuality'?
4. Is embodiment a key feature of the digital age?
5. What is the 'posthuman'?

ANNOTATED GUIDE TO FURTHER READING

I INTRODUCTION: CONCEPTS AND MEDIA

Giles Deleuze and Félix Guattari, *What is Philosophy?* The first chapter of this book – 'What is a Concept?' – is key reading. It declares that concepts underpin all meaningful philosophical work. This is a challenging text, but one that repays close study.

Jean Baudrillard, *Passwords*. This book is an attempt to turn concepts into passwords that can be used to gain access to the underlying value-systems of culture today. This is a high-level philosophical work, and is more accessible when read alongside the Baudrillard texts encountered in **Chapter 7**.

Martin Lister et al., *New Media: A Critical Introduction*. This introductory text outlines a number of key characteristics of, and critical approaches to, new media technologies. It is a useful resource for those encountering the subject for the first time.

Jay Bolter and Richard Grusin, *Remediation: Understanding New Media*. This is a sophisticated work that questions whether many of the attributes of so-called new media are in fact 'new'. It argues that new visual media refashion or 'remediate' earlier media such as painting, photography, film and television.

2 NETWORK

Manuel Castells, *The Rise of the Network Society*. This is the first volume of Castells' famous trilogy *The Information Age*. It is key reading for students interested in the 'networked' basis of contemporary society and culture. The chapters on 'The Space of Flows' and 'Timeless Time' have been particularly influential in the field of new media studies, and are worth close study.

Giles Deleuze and Félix Guattari, *A Thousand Plateaus*. This is one of the most inventive and challenging philosophical works of the late twentieth century. Its opening chapter, entitled 'Rhizome', has been used by many to think theoretically about the dynamics and topologies of new media networks. This is a book for the advanced reader.

Tiziana Terranova, *Network Culture*. This is an advanced but accessible book that draws on information and cybernetic theory to theorize media networks. It treats the Internet as a self-organizing system, and asks of the possibility of politics in an age of 'media saturation' and 'information overload'.

Alex Galloway, *Protocol: How Control Exists After Decentralization*. This book examines the technical protocols of the Internet in order to suggest that its networks are founded upon control rather than freedom. The text is inspired by the writings of Deleuze but is accessible to a student audience.

3 INFORMATION

Hans Christian von Baeyer, *Information: The New Language of Science*. For those looking for an overview of different scientific and philosophical approaches to the study of information, this is a good place to start.

Claude Shannon and Warren Weaver, *The Mathematical Theory of Communication*. This is the classic text of early information science and cybernetic theory. Given its mathematical orientation it is more likely to appeal to students of computer science, but many of its key ideas underpin contemporary media theory. It is a dense, technical work, and uninitiated readers are advised to start with the essay by Weaver that forms the first part of this volume.

Jean-François Lyotard, *The Postmodern Condition*. This now infamous text suggests that information is becoming *the* key commodity of advanced capitalist societies. The introduction by Fredric Jameson is helpful for those reading Lyotard for the first time.

Scott Lash, *Critique of Information*. This is a wide-ranging book that centres on the emergence of new technological forms of life and being. It addresses the immediacy of information order, and considers the possibility of information critique. It is likely to appeal to the advanced reader.

4 INTERFACE

Steven Johnson, *Interface Culture: How New Technology Transforms the Way We Create and Communicate*. This is a useful student-friendly introduction to the study of interfaces.

Donna Haraway, *Simians, Cyborgs and Women: The Reinvention of Nature*. This advanced text addresses the interfacing of a range of human, animal and machinic systems. It also forges key concepts of information, informatics and embodiment that we consider in **Chapters 3** and **7**.

Wilbert Galitz, *The Essential Guide to User Interface Design: An Introduction to GUI Design Principles and Techniques*. This is a useful text for those wanting to explore the technical underpinnings of interface design.

Sherry Turkle, *Evocative Objects: Things We Think With*. This wide-ranging collection of essays looks at the interface between objects and our emotions and thoughts. It is clearly written and is accessible to a student audience.

5 ARCHIVE

Jacques Derrida, *Archive Fever: A Freudian Impression*. This work, while only marginally connected to the study of new media archives, is a key point of departure for theoretical analysis of contemporary archival technologies. It is a difficult and challenging text that presumes some knowledge of psychoanalytic theory.

Mike Featherstone, 'Archiving Cultures'. This paper was one of the first to look at changes in the production and recording of culture following the emergence of 'electronic archives', and is still a common point of reference today.

Joke Brouwer and Arjun Mulder (eds), *Information is Alive: Art and Theory on Archiving and Retrieving Data*. This collection, produced by the V2 Institute for Unstable Media, brings together figures from art theory, sociology and cultural studies to consider the transformation of archives in the digital age.

Yochai Benkler, *The Wealth of Networks*. The focus of this lengthy book is the 'networked information economy', including new forms of 'peer production'. It extends contemporary debates around Web 2.0, intellectual property rights and open forms of collaboration that we address only in brief in this chapter.

6 INTERACTIVITY

Marshall McLuhan, *Understanding Media*. This book is essential reading for students working within the fields of media or cultural studies. At surface level this is an easy text to read, but many of McLuhan's propositions are more complex than they first appear, including the idea that media may be classified as either hot or cool.

Lev Manovich, *The Language of New Media*. In this work, Manovich questions the assumption that new media are interactive by definition, and the idea that media interactivity can be reduced to a single type. This is essential reading, particularly for those with a technical interest in new media systems.

Nigel Thrift, *Knowing Capitalism*. Thrift ties new media to the emergence of new forms of 'virtual' or 'soft' capitalism that are ever more intelligent or 'knowing'. Of interest here is the idea that interactivity is a form of technical play or seduction that is increasingly of value to the capitalist market.

Andrew Barry, *Political Machines: Governing a Technological Society*. This book examines the political rhetoric of interactivity, and argues that it is wedded to a new ideal of active citizenship. It addresses a range of connections between power and technology, and is likely to be of interest to students of the social and political sciences.

7 SIMULATION

Jean Baudrillard, *Symbolic Exchange and Death*. This, alongside *Simulacra and Simulation*, is Baudrillard's key work on simulation, and is where he develops his notion of the hyperreal. This is difficult but essential reading.

Nicholas Perry, *Hyperreality and Global Culture*. This is an accessible text that demonstrates how concepts of simulation and hyperreality might be applied to the study of global culture.

Katherine N. Hayles, *My Mother Was a Computer*. Hayles's *How We Became Posthuman* forwards an argument for the embodiment of information by engaging with three generations of cybernetic theory. *My Mother Was a Computer* takes this project further by considering the 'intermediation' of language and code in everyday life. This is a text for the advanced reader.

Friedrich Kittler. *Literature, Media, Information Systems*. This collection of essays and book chapters offers a wide-ranging introduction to the writings of Friedrich Kittler. It contains two essays in particular that demand close study in relation to the question of simulation: 'There is No Software' and 'Protected Mode'.

BIBLIOGRAPHY

Agger, B. (1991). *Fast Capitalism*. Urbana: University of Illinois Press.

Agger, B. (2004). *Speeding Up Fast Capitalism*. Boulder, CO: Paradigm.

Appadurai, A. (1996). *Modernity At Large: Cultural Dimensions of Globalization*. Minneapolis: University of Minnesota Press.

Appadurai, A. (2003). 'Archive and Inspiration', in J. Brouwer and A. Mulder (eds), *Information is Alive*. Rotterdam: V2/NAi.

Barry, A. (2001). *Political Machines: Governing a Technological Society*. London: Athlone.

Baudrillard, J. (1983). *In the Shadow of the Silent Majorities*. New York: Semiotext(e).

Baudrillard, J. (1993a). *Symbolic Exchange and Death*. London: Sage.

Baudrillard, J. (1993b). *The Transparency of Evil*. London: Verso.

Baudrillard, J. (1994). *Simulacra and Simulation*. Ann Arbor: University of Michigan Press.

Baudrillard, J. (2002). *The Spirit of Terrorism*. London: Verso.

Baudrillard, J. (2003). *Passwords*. London: Verso.

Baudrillard, J. (2004). *The Gulf War Did Not Take Place*. Sydney: Power.

Bauman, Z. (1998). *Globalization: The Human Consequences*. Cambridge: Polity.

Bauman, Z. (2000). *Liquid Modernity*. Cambridge: Polity.

Bauman, Z. (2001a). *Community*. Cambridge: Polity.

Bauman, Z. (2001b). *The Individualized Society*. Cambridge: Polity.

Beck, U. (2000). 'The Cosmopolitan Perspective', *British Journal of Sociology* 51(1): 79–105.

Beck, U. (2002). 'The Cosmopolitan Society and its Enemies', *Theory, Culture & Society* 19(1–2): 17–44.

Beer, D. (2006). 'The Pop-Pickers Have Picked Decentralised Media: The Fall of Top of the Pops and the Rise of the Second Media Age', *Sociological Research Online* 11(3): http://www.socresonline.org.uk/11/3/beer.html

Beer, D. (2007). 'Thoughtful Territories: Imagining the Thinking Power of Things and Spaces', *City* 11(2): 229–38.

Beer, D. (2008). 'The iConic iNterface and the Veneer of Simplicity: The MP3 Player and the Reconfiguration of Music Collecting and Reproduction Practices in the Digital Age', *Information, Communication & Society* 11(1): 71–88.

Beer, D. and Burrows, R. (2007). 'Sociology and, of and in Web 2.0: Some Initial Considerations'. *Sociological Research Online*, 12(5): http://www.socresonline.org.uk/12/5/17.html.

Bell, D. (1976). *The Coming of Post-Industrial Society*. New York: Basic.

Benkler, Y. (2006). *The Wealth of Networks: How Social Production Transforms Markets and Freedom*. New Haven, CT: Yale University Press.

Berlin, I. (1980). *Concepts and Categories: Philosophical Essays*. Oxford: Oxford University Press.

Bolter, J. and Grusin, R. (1999). *Remediation: Understanding New Media*. Cambridge, MA: MIT Press.

Bott, E. (1957). *Family and Social Network: Roles, Norms, and External Relationships in Ordinary Urban Families*. London: Tavistock.

Bowker, G.C. and Star, S.L. (1999) *Sorting Things Out: Classification and Its Consequences*. Cambridge, MA: MIT Press.

Brouwer, J. and Mulder, A. (2003). 'Information is Alive', in J. Brouwer and A. Mulder (eds), *Information is Alive: Art and Theory on Archiving and Retrieving Data*. Rotterdam: V2/NAi.

Burger, T. (1976). *Max Weber's Theory of Concept Formation: History, Laws and Ideal Types*. Durham, NC: Duke University Press.

Burrows, R. (1997). 'Cyberpunk as Social Theory: William Gibson and the Sociological Imagination', in S. Westwood and J. Williams (eds), *Imagining Cities: Scripts, Signs and Memories*. London: Routledge.

Burrows, R. and Ellison, N. (2004) 'Sorting Places Out? Towards a Social Politics of Neighbourhood Informatization', *Information, Communication & Society* 7(3): 321–36.

Burrows, R and Gane, N. (2006). 'Geodemographics, Software and Class'. *Sociology* 40(5): 793–812.

Castells, M. (1996). *The Rise of the Network Society. The Information Age: Economy, Society and Culture*, Vol. 1. Oxford: Blackwell.

Castells, M. (1997). *The Power of Identity. The Information Age: Economy, Society and Culture*, Vol. 2. Oxford: Blackwell.

Castells, M. (2000a). *End of Millennium. The Information Age: Economy, Society and Culture*, Vol. 3. Oxford: Blackwell.

Castells, M. (2000b). 'Materials for an Exploratory Theory of the Network Society'. *British Journal of Sociology* 51(1): 5–24.

Castells, M. (2001). *The Internet Galaxy*. Oxford: Oxford University Press.

Caygill, H. (1999). 'Meno and the Internet: Between Memory and the Archive', *History of the Human Sciences* 12(2): 1–11.

Comer, D. (2004). *Computer Networks and Internets*. Upper Saddle River, NJ: Pearson Prentice Hall.

Crang, M., Crosbie, T. and Graham, S. (2006). 'Variable Geometries of Connection: Urban Digital Divides and the Uses of Information Technology', *Urban Studies* 43(13): 2551–70.

Crang, M. and Graham, S. (2007). 'Sentient Cities: Ubiquitous Computing and the Politics of Urban Space', *Information, Communication & Society* 10(6): 789–817.

Cubitt, S. (2001). *Simulation and Social Theory*. London: Sage.

Damasio, A. (2003). 'The Memory as Living Archive', in J. Brouwer and A. Mulder (eds), *Information is Alive*. Rotterdam: V2/NAi.

DeLanda, M. (2003). 'The Archive Before and After Foucault', in J. Brouwer and A. Mulder (eds), *Information is Alive*. Rotterdam: V2/NAi.

DeLanda, M. (2006). *A New Philosophy of Society: Assemblage Theory and Social Complexity*. London and New York: Continuum.

Deleuze, G. and Guattari, F. (1987). *A Thousand Plateaus: Capitalism and Schizophrenia*. Minneapolis: University of Minnesota Press.

Deleuze, G. and Guattari, F. (1994). *What is Philosophy?* New York: Columbia University Press.

Delorie, D. (nd.). 'Guide: What does protected mode mean?'. http://www.delorie.com/djgpp/doc/ug/basics/protected.html.

Der Derian, J. (2001). *Virtuous War*. Boulder, CO: Westview.

Derrida, J. (1996). *Archive Fever: A Freudian Impression*. Chicago: University of Chicago Press.

Derrida, J. (2001). *Writing and Difference*. London and New York: Routledge.

de Souza e Silva, A. (2006). 'From Cyber to Hybrid: Mobile Technologies as Interfaces of Hybrid Spaces', *Space and Culture* 9(3): 261–78.

Dicks, B., Mason, D., Coffey, A. and Atkinson, P. (2005). *Qualitative Research and Hypermedia: Ethnography for the Digital Age*. London: Sage.

Drysdale, J. (1996). 'How are Social-Scientific Concepts Formed? A Reconstruction of Max Weber's Theory of Concept Formation'. *Sociological Theory* 14(1): 71–88.

Eco, U. (1989). *The Open Work*. Cambridge, MA: Harvard University Press.

Featherstone, M. (2000). 'Archiving Cultures'. *British Journal of Sociology* 51(1): 161–84.

Featherstone, M. (2006). 'Archive', *Theory, Culture & Society* 23(2–3): 591–6.

Feldman, T. (1997). *Introduction to Digital Media*. London: Routledge.

Fernández-Armesto, F. (2004). *So You Think You're Human?* Oxford and New York: Oxford University Press.

Foucault, M. (1970). *The Order of Things*. London: Routledge.

Foucault, M. (1972). *The Archaeology of Knowledge*. London: Routledge.

Freud, S. (1991 [1925]). *General Psychological Theory*. New York: Simon & Schuster.

Fukuyama, F. (2002). *Our Posthuman Future*. London: Profile.

Galitz, W. (2007). *The Essential Guide to User Interface Design: An Introduction to GUI Design Principles and Techniques*. Hoboken, NJ: Wiley.

Galloway, Alex. (2004). *Protocol: How Control Exists After Decentralization*. Cambridge, MA: MIT Press.

Galloway, Alex. (2006). 'Protocol'. *Theory, Culture & Society* 23(2–3): 317–20.

Galloway, Anne. (2004). 'Intimations of Everyday Life: Ubiquitous Computing and the City', *Cultural Studies* 18(2/3): 384–408.

Gane, N. (2003). Computerized Capitalism: The Media Theory of Jean-François Lyotard'. *Information, Communication & Society* 6(3): 430–50.

Gane, N. (2004). *The Future of Social Theory*. London: Continuum.

Gane, N. (2005a). 'Radical Posthumanism: Friedrich Kittler and the Primacy of Technology'. *Theory, Culture & Society* 22(3): 25–41.

Gane, N. (2005b). 'An Information Age Without Technology?: A Response to Webster'. *Information, Communication & Society* 8(4): 471–6.

Gane, N. (2006). 'Speed up or slow down? Social Theory in the Information Age'. *Information, Communication & Society* 9(1): 20–38.

Gane, N. and Haraway, D. (2006). 'When We Have Never Been Human, What is To Be Done?' *Theory, Culture & Society* 23(7–8): 135–58.

Gane, N., Venn, C. and Hand, M. (2007). 'Ubiquitous Surveillance: Interview with Katherine Hayles'. *Theory, Culture & Society* 24(7–8): 349–58.

Garton, L., Haythornthwaite, C. and Wellman, B. (1999). 'Studying On-Line Social Networks', in S. Jones (ed.), *Doing Internet Research*. London: Sage, pp. 75–104.

Gibson, W. (2003). *Pattern Recognition*. London: Penguin.

Graham, S. (2004). 'From Dreams of Transcendence to the Remediation of Urban Life', in S. Graham (ed.), *The Cybercities Reader*. London: Routledge.

Graham, S. and Marvin, S. (2001). *Splintering Urbanism: Networked Infrastructures, Technological Mobilities and the Urban Condition*. London and New York: Routledge.

Habermas, J. (1984). *The Theory of Communicative Action*, 2 vols. Cambridge: Polity.

Halberstam, J. and Livingstone, I. (eds) (1995). *Posthuman Bodies*. Bloomington and Indianapolis: Indiana University Press.

Hannoum, A. (2005). 'Paul Ricoeur On Memory'. *Theory, Culture & Society* 22(6): 123–37.

Haraway, D. (1991). *Simians, Cyborgs, and Women: The Reinvention of Nature*. London: Free Association.

Haraway, D. (1997). Modest_Witness@Second_Millennium. FemaleMan©_Meets_Oncomouse™. London: Routlege.

Haraway, D. (2004). *The Haraway Reader*. London: Routledge.

Hardey, M. and Burrows, R. (2008). 'New Cartographies of *Knowing* Capitalism and the Changing Jurisdictions of Empirical Sociology', in N. Fielding, R.M. Lee, and G. Blank (eds), *Handbook of Internet and Online Research Methods*. London: Sage.

Hayles, N.K. (1998) 'How Does It Feel To Be Posthuman?' http://framework.v2.nl/archive/archive/node/text/default.xslt/nodenr-70187

Hayles, N.K. (1999). *How We Became Posthuman: Virtual Bodies in Cybernetics, Literature, and Informatics*. Chicago: University of Chicago Press.

Hayles, N.K. (2002). *Writing Machines*. Cambridge, MA: MIT Press.

Hayles, N.K. (2005a). *My Mother Was a Computer: Digital Subjects and Literary Texts*. Chicago: University of Chicago Press.

Hayles, N.K. (2005b). 'Computing the Human'. *Theory, Culture & Society* 22(1): 131–51.

Hayles, N.K. (2006). 'Unfinished Work: From Cyborg to Cognisphere'. *Theory, Culture & Society* 23(7–8): 159–66.

Hine, C. (2000). *Virtual Ethnography*. London: Sage.

Idhe, D. (1979). *Technics and Praxis*. London: D. Reidel.

Idhe, D. (1990). *Technology and the Lifeworld: From Garden to Earth*. Bloomington: Indiana University Press.

Illingworth, V. and Pyle, I. (2004). *Dictionary of Computing*. Oxford: Oxford University Press.

Johnson, S. (1997). *Interface Culture: How New Technology Transforms the Way We Create and Communicate*. New York: Basic Books.

Johnston, J. (1997). 'Friedrich Kittler: Media Theory After Poststructuralism', in F. Kittler, *Literature, Media, Information Systems*. Amsterdam: G+B Arts.

Keen, A. (2007). *The Cult of the Amateur: How Today's Internet Is Killing Our Culture and Assaulting Our Economy*. Boston and London: Nicholas Brealey.

Kiousis, S. (2002). 'Interactivity: a Concept Explication', *New Media & Society* 4(3): 355–83.

Kirkpatrick, G. (2004). *Critical Technology: A Social Theory of Personal Computing*. Aldershot: Ashgate.

Kittler, F. (1986). 'A Discourse on Discourse'. *Stanford Literary Review* 3(1): 157–66.

Kittler, F. (1990). *Discourse Networks 1800/1900*. Stanford, CA: Stanford University Press.

Kittler, F. (1992). 'Spooky Electricity'. *Artforum*, December: 66–70.

Kittler, F. (1993). *Draculas Vermächtnis: Technische Schriften*. Leipzig: Reclam.

Kittler, F. (1996). 'Technologies of Writing/Rewriting Technology'. *New Literary History* 27(4): 731–42.

Kittler, F. (1997). *Literature, Media, Information Systems*. Amsterdam: G+B Arts.

Kittler, F. (1999). *Gramophone, Film, Typewriter*. Stanford, CA: Stanford University Press.

Kittler, F. and Virilio, P. (2001). 'The Information Bomb: A Conversation', in J. Armitage (ed.), *Virilio Live*. London: Sage.

Kittler, F. (2002). *Optische Medien*. Berlin: Merve.

Klein, N. (2000). *No Logo*. London: HarperCollins.

Knox, H., Savage, M. and Harvey, P. (2006). 'Social Networks and the Study of Relations: Networks as Method, Metaphor and Form'. *Economy and Society* 35(1): 113–40.

Kuhn, T. (1996). *The Structure of Scientific Revolutions*. Chicago: University of Chicago Press.

Lacan, J. (1988). *The Seminar of Jacques Lacan Book II: The Ego in Freud's Theory and the Technique of Psychoanalysis 1954–1955*. Cambridge: Cambridge University Press.

Lash, S. (2002). *Critique of Information*. London: Sage.

Lash, S. (2007). 'Power after Hegemony: Cultural Studies in Mutation'. *Theory, Culture & Society* 24(3): 55–78.

Latour, B. (1999). 'On Recalling ANT', in J. Law and J. Hassard (eds), *Actor Network Theory and After*. Oxford: Blackwell.

Latour, B. (2000). 'When Things Strike Back: A Possible Contribution of "Science Studies" to the Social Sciences'. *British Journal of Sociology* 51(1): 107–24.

Latour, B. (2002). 'Gabriel Tarde and the End of the Social', in P. Joyce (ed.), *The Social in Question*. London: Routledge.

Latour, B. (2005). *Reassembling the Social: An Introduction to Actor-Network-Theory*. Oxford: Oxford University Press.

Law, J. (1999). 'After ANT: Complexity, Naming and Topology', in J. Law and J. Hassard (eds) *Actor Network Theory and After*. Oxford: Blackwell.

Law, J. and Hassard, J. (eds) (1999). *Actor Network Theory and After*. Oxford: Blackwell.

Lessig, L. (2004). *Free Culture*. London and New York: Penguin.

Lessig, L. (2006). *Code: Version 2.0*. New York: Basic.

Lister, M. et al. (2003). *New Media: A Critical Introduction*. London: Routledge.

Loader, B. (ed.) (1998). *Cyberspace Divide: Equality, Agency and Policy in the Information Society*. London: Routledge.

Loader, B. and Keeble, L. (2004). *Challenging the Digital Divide?: A Literature Review of Community Informatics Initiatives*. York: Joseph Rowntree Foundation.

Lovink, G. (ed.) (2002). *Uncanny Networks: Dialogues with the Virtual Intelligentsia*. Cambridge, MA: MIT Press.

Lynch, M. (1999). 'Archives in Formation: Privileged Spaces, Popular Archives and Paper Trails'. *History of the Human Sciences* 12(2): 65–87.

Lyotard, J.-F. (1984). *The Postmodern Condition: A Report on Knowledge*. Manchester: Manchester University Press.

Lyotard, J.-F. (1993). *The Inhuman: Reflections on Time*. Cambridge: Polity.

Machlup, P. (1962). *The Production and Distribution of Knowledge in the United States*. Princeton, NJ: Princeton University Press.

Manovich, L. (2001). *The Language of New Media*. Cambridge, MA: MIT Press.

Mattelart, A. (2003). *The Information Society: An Introduction*. London: Sage.

McLuhan, M. (1964). *Understanding Media*. London: Routledge.

McLuhan, M. and Fiore, Q. (1967). *The Medium is the Massage*. New York: Bantam.

Milner, S. (1999). 'Partial Readings Addressing a Renaissance Archive'. *History of the Human Sciences* 12(2): 89–105.

Mitchell, W.J. (2003). *ME++: The Cyborg Self and the Networked City*. Cambridge, MA: MIT Press.

Mitchell, W.J. (2005). *Placing Words: Symbols, Space, and the City*. Cambridge, MA: MIT Press.

Moravec, H. (1999). *Robot: Mere Machine to Transcendent Mind*. Oxford: Oxford University Press.

Negroponte, N. (1996). *Being Digital*. New York: Vintage.

Nettleton, S., Burrows, R., O'Malley, L. and Watt, I. (2005). 'Health e-Types? An Analysis of the Everyday Use of the Internet for Health'. *Information, Communication & Society* 7(4): 531–53.

Neustadtl, A., Robinson, J.P. and Kestnbaum, M. (2002). 'Doing Social Science Research Online', in B. Wellman and C. Haythornthwaite (eds), *The Internet in Everyday Life*. Oxford: Blackwell.

Oakes, G. (1988). *Weber and Rickert: Concept Formation in the Cultural Sciences*. Cambridge, MA: MIT Press.

O'Hara, K. and Stevens, D. (2006). *Inequality.Com: Power, Poverty and the Digital Divide*. Oxford: One World.

O'Reilly, T. (2005). 'What is Web 2.0: Design Patterns and Business Models for the Next Generation of Software', *O'Reilly*, http://oreillynet.com/1pt/a/6228 (7 December 2006).

Osborne, T. (1999). 'The Ordinariness of the Archive', *History of the Human Sciences* 12(2): 51–64.

Ostrow, S. (1997). 'Friedrich Kittler: The Passage from Network to Narrative', in F. Kittler, *Literature, Media, Information Systems*. Amsterdam: G + B Arts.

Pepperell, R. (2003). *The Posthuman Condition*. Bristol and Portland: Intellect.

Perry, M. and Oskov, N. (nd.). 'Introduction to Reverse Engineering Software'. http://www.acm.uiuc.edu/sigmil/RevEng/ch01.html.

Perry, N. (1998). *Hyperreality and Global Culture*. London: Routledge.

Porat, M. (1977). *The Information Economy: Definition and Measurement*. Washington, DC: US Department of Commerce.

Poster, M. (1996). *The Second Media Age*. Cambridge: Polity Press.

Reading, A. (2003). 'Digital Interactivity in Public Memory Institutions: the Uses of New Technologies in Holocaust Museums'. *Media, Culture & Society* 25(1): 67–85.

Rheingold, H. (2000). *Virtual Community*. Cambridge, MA: MIT Press.

Ritzer, G. (2003). *The Globalization of Nothing*. Thousand Oaks: Pine Forge.

Ritzer, G. (2007). 'Theorizing Web 2.0'. Unpublished paper presented at Towards a Social Science of Web 2.0 Conference, University of York, 6 September 2007.

Savage, M., Bagnall, G. and Longhurst, B. (2005). *Globalisation and Belonging*. London: Sage.

Savage, M. and Burrows, R. (2007). 'The Coming Crisis of Empirical Sociology', *Sociology* 41(5): 885–99.

Scott, J. (2000). *Social Network Analysis: A Handbook*, 2nd edn. London: Sage.

Schultz, T. (2000). 'Mass Media and the Concept of Interactivity: An Exploratory Study of Online Forums and Reader Email', *Media, Culture & Society* 22(2): 205–21.

Shannon, C. and Weaver, W. (1949). *The Mathematical Theory of Communication*. Urbana: University of Illinois Press.

Shay, W. (1999). *Understanding Data Communications and Networks*. Pacific Grove, CA: Brooks Cole.

Silverstone, R. (1999). 'What's New About New Media?', *New Media & Society* 1(1): 10–82.

Steedman, C. (2001). 'Something She Called a Fever: Michelet, Derrida, and Dust'. *American Historical Review* 106(4): 4–19.

Sterne, J. (2003). *The Audible Past: Cultural Origins of Sound Reproduction*. Durham, NC: Duke University Press.

Terranova, T. (2004). *Network Culture: Politics for the Information Age*. London: Pluto.

Terranova, T. (2006). 'The Concept of Information'. *Theory, Culture & Society* 23(2): 286–8.

Thrift, N. (2005). *Knowing Capitalism*. London: Sage.

Turkle, S.(ed.) (2007). *Evocative Objects: Things We Think With*. Cambridge, MA: MIT Press.

Turow, J. (2006). *Niche Envy: Marketing Discrimination in the Digital Age*. Cambridge, MA: MIT Press.

Urry, J. (2000). *Sociology Beyond Societies*. London: Routledge.

Urry, J. (2003). *Global Complexity*. Cambridge: Polity.

van Loon, J. (2006). 'Network'. *Theory, Culture & Society* 23(2–3): 307–14.

Virilio, P. (1998). *Pure War*. New York: Semiotext(e).

von Baeyer, H. (2003). *Information: The New Language of Science*. Cambridge, MA: Harvard University Press.

Waldby, C. (2000). *The Visible Human Project: Informatic Bodies and Posthuman Medicine*. London and New York: Routledge.

Walrand, J. (1998). *Communication Networks*. Boston: McGraw-Hill.

Webster, F. (2002). *Theories of the Information Society*. London: Routledge.

Wellberry, D. (1990). 'Foreword', in F. Kittler, *Discourse Networks 1800/1900*. Stanford, CA: Stanford University Press.

Wellman, B. and Berkowitz, S. (1988). *Social Structures: A Network Approach*. Cambridge: Cambridge University Press.

Wellman, B. and Gulia, M. (1999). 'Net Surfers Don't Ride Alone: Virtual Communities as Communities', in B. Wellman (ed.), *Network in the Global Village*. Boulder, CO: Westview.

Wellman, B. and Haythornthwaite, C. (eds) (2002). *The Internet in Everyday Life*. Oxford: Blackwell.

White, H. (1988). 'Varieties of Markets', in B. Wellman and S. Berkowitz (eds) *Social Structures: A Network Approach*. Cambridge: Cambridge University Press.

Woolgar, S. (2002). 'Five Rules of Virtuality', in S. Woolgar (ed.), *Virtual Society? Technology, Cyberbole, Reality*. Oxford : Oxford University Press, pp. 1–22.

Yoshimi, S. (2006). 'Information'. *Theory, Culture & Society* 23(2): 271–8.

INDEX